The Psychology of
Political Extremism

The Psychology of Political Extremism

What would Sigmund Freud have thought about Islamic State?

Gabrielle Rifkind

Warmest wishes
Gabrielle

Routledge
Taylor & Francis Group

LONDON AND NEW YORK

First published 2018
by Routledge
2 Park Square, Milton Park, Abingdon, Oxon OX14 4RN

and by Routledge
711 Third Avenue, New York, NY 10017

Routledge is an imprint of the Taylor & Francis Group, an informa business

British Library Cataloguing-in-Publication Data
A catalogue record for this book is available from the British Library

Library of Congress Cataloging-in-Publication Data
A catalog record has been requested for this book

ISBN: 9–781–78220–663–7 (pbk)

Edited, designed, and typeset in Quay Sans EF and Adobe Caslon Pro by Communication Crafts, East Grinstead

Printed by CPI Group (UK) Ltd, Croydon CR0 4YY

CONTENTS

Gabrielle Rifkind is a practising psychotherapist and a group analyst and a specialist in the resolution of conflict. She has spent the past two decades working in conflict resolution in the Middle East. She has recently established and directs the Oxford Process (www.oxfordprocess.com), a conflict-mediation initiative that works quietly behind the scenes to prevent countries tipping into conflict or, when war has broken out, helping to ripen the conditions for peace-making. She combines in-depth political knowledge and psychological expertise with many years' experience of promoting serious analysis and discreet dialogues with groups behind the scenes.

In her last book, *The Fog of Peace: How to Prevent War* (2014), co-authored with veteran UN negotiator Gian-domenico Picco, Rifkind argues that we need a radical new approach to the international resolution of conflict and that the primary aim in any international intervention should be to contain violence and provide a framework for negotiations before conflict escalates.

In her current book, *The Psychology of Political Extremism: What Would Sigmund Freud Have Thought About Islamic State?*,

Rifkind argues that Islamic State is seen primarily through a political lens: the psychological motivation of such groups is poorly understood. But we need to ask the question, do the inner disquiets of Islam make more sense to the psychologists than to the imams?

Recent terrorist attacks have left the United Kingdom genuinely at sea as to how to respond to these distressing events. There are the predictable interpretations, with politicians on the right talking about counterterrorism, harsher punishments, and tightening up on the Internet, while on the political left there is talk about blaming foreign wars. All this analysis is relevant, but insufficient. Politicians are not talking about why so many young people in this country are sufficiently angry and alienated that they are prepared to be seduced by the toxic and poisonous ideology of Islamic State. This book examines both the politics and the psychology and what motivates people to behave in ways that are so disturbing. Freud is the hook as the founding father of the talking cure. A radical and subversive theorist in his time, he claimed that mankind was influenced more by the inner workings of the mind and internal conflicts than by rational thought.

Rifkind makes regular contributions to the media, including *The Guardian, Independent, The Times*, and radio and television. She has appeared on various news and political analysis programmes, given many public lectures, and engaged in debates at venues ranging from the Oxford Union to the House of Commons, to Princeton University. She has recently been the conflict mediator on the Radio 4 series, "Across the Red Line". She lives in London.

The Psychology of
Political Extremism

ONE
Freud, the father of psychoanalysis

Sigmund Freud warned in 1915 that the "primitive, savage and evil impulses of mankind have not vanished in any individual", but are simply waiting for the opportunity to show themselves (Fiebig-von Has & Lehmkuhl, 1997, p. 5). This reflected his view that lurking inside every human being was the capacity to be destructive. Amplified at a state level, this explained man's likelihood to go to war. Freud lived and wrote during a period of fascist darkness in Europe, and his work was to inspire many analysts to believe that "knowledge of the unconscious could contribute to making a better, more democratic world" (Pick, 2012, p. 2). His essential message was that the better we know ourselves, the less likely we are to go to war.

This book addresses the rise of Islamic State and explores whether Islamic State is an entirely new phenomenon or a mirror of a troubled Middle East region at war with itself. Does this terrorist organisation (and others like it) speak to a wider global phenomenon of a world ill at ease with itself? Islamic State is primarily seen through a political lens; the psychological motivation of such groups is poorly understood. But we need to ask the question, "do the inner disquiets of Islam make more sense to the psychologists than to the imams?" (Bellaigue, 2017).

This book provides an opportunity to explore these questions. Freud will be the hook for this analysis, as the founding father of the talking cure. A radical and subversive theorist in his time, he was to claim that mankind was influenced more by the inner workings of the mind and internal conflicts than by rational thought. Many of his ideas did not receive a warm reception at the time. He was accused of descending into the "spiritual gutter; with such ideas belonging in prison" (Kahr, 2017). He challenged the way that society thought about itself in his commitment to understanding not just behaviour, but what was going on beneath the surface.

If we apply this analysis to the emergence of Islamic State, it will require that we do not just see them as a barbaric group. We will need to understand them in the context of Middle East politics and consider how they have emerged out of the horrors of war. We will also need to understand the psychic disturbances within the individual, the group, and the state. It will be necessary to differentiate between those who join Islamic State from within the region, those who join from abroad, and those whose strategy involves making attacks on home soil. There will be multiple motivations driving the problems, but often the inner workings of the mind are forgotten.

At the time of the initial stages of writing this book, the main focus was the rise of Islamic State and the surge of foreign fighters who go abroad to fight for these groups. Now the focus has moved to the attacks on mainland Europe. Britain's large cities are facing an ever-increasing threat from those who identify with jihadi extremist groups. More recently, there were three disturbing and tragic terrorist attacks; there will probably be more before this book is published and read.

The country is genuinely at sea as to how to respond to these distressing events. There are the predictable interpretations, with politicians on the right talking about counterterrorism, harsher punishments, and tightening up on the Internet, while the political left is blaming foreign wars. All this analysis is relevant, but it is insufficient. Politicians are not talking about why so many young people are sufficiently angry and alienated that they are prepared to be seduced by the toxic and poisonous ideology of Islamic State. For this reason, the aim of this book is not just to examine the politics, but to provide a better understanding of the mindset that motivates these people to behave in ways that are so disturbing.

On the wider political stage, it will challenge us to think about whether we are again entering a new period of darkness and to consider whether we know enough about human behaviour to avoid this fate. It leads us to ask the question of why "ordinary human beings resort to war and kill each other when under different conditions they would rather go and visit their grandmother or take their children to school" (Rifkind & Picco, 2014, p. xv). What is it about human behaviour that unleashes a terrible ferment of war and magnifies the worst aspects of human nature?

Freud believed that self-knowledge, which could be applied both to the individual and to the state, could help limit our potential for destruction. Many of his insights will be relevant a hundred years later. But some of his ideas and how they are framed are culture-specific, reflecting both the political era in which he was writing and the limitations of his European lens. He was a citizen of the early twentieth century – a time when Europe was both ethnocentric and xenophobic. Accordingly, "Freud himself had a degree of European ethnocentrism and a tendency to stereotype and denigrate other cultures" (Volkan, 2014, p. 17).

My own background is as a group analyst, psychotherapist, and art therapist. A very strange hybrid, I have worked in the field of conflict resolution in the Middle East for the last two decades. My motivation has been shaped by a deep belief that one of the reasons that we both create and fail to resolve war is that war is understood through the lens of *realpolitik*, which is about power. This paradigm does not sufficiently recognise human motivation and why people behave in particular ways. Without these insights, it is difficult to both prevent and resolve war. One of the basic assumptions of this book is that young people who are attracted to Islamic State are driven by both psychological and political motivations: we would do well to understand both. Currently the emphasis is on the latter, with scant commitment to understanding the psychological.

As a psychotherapist, working for more than three decades with individuals and groups, I have learnt a great deal about conflict of the marital rather than the military kind. I never dreamed at the start of my career that I would be transposing my skills from the consulting room to the Middle East. My route from a comfortable therapy room in North London to the less salubrious setting of a sparsely furnished Damascus flat, where, with me as the only woman, we would travel to secret destinations to meet the leadership of Hamas and have other clandestine meetings, was not the conventional trajectory of a psychotherapist's career. All the while under armed guard, I had a growing sense that the old military interventions were no longer enough. That without a deeper psychological understanding of the issues at stake, and without a new language with which to explore them, the old cycles of violence would continue indefinitely.

So politics and psychotherapy were to become my main diet and the intertwining of my two passions. Being a psychotherapist offers you an extraordinary entry into people's lives: their hopes, their fears, their humiliations, their hidden secrets, but most of all what motivates them, what they care about, and how they think. I became hungry to draw on these skills in order to develop the links between the psychological and the political worlds. Over the past decade, I have worked on applying what I know psychologically to the political process – by this I mean our understanding of what stimulates conflict; what makes people act either destructively or creatively; and what leads people to become so entrenched in their hatred that they will continue to fight, whatever the cost.

Given the current preoccupation with political violence, my aim was to deepen my knowledge of what motivates such behaviour, not in order to excuse it but to develop a deeper understanding of its root causes and thereby forge a more considered path of response and possible intervention. I had to look beyond the symptom of political violence and understand the causes, which, in some instances, may have been marginalisation, dehumanisation, and humiliation. While I have an instinctive abhorrence of violence, it may also be understood as an autistic communication – a non-verbal one that does not address the real issues that offer the possibility of change or resolution of conflict.

While politics is not about therapy, and politicians and states cannot be placed on the couch, human motivation and psychology needs to be part of the strategic calculations of decision makers. For "it is man who both creates and ends wars, and destroys his environment. Institutions do not decide who to destroy or kill, or make peace or war; those actions are the responsibility of individuals" (Rifkind & Picco, 2014, p. 3). So trying to understand the root causes of conflict only in terms of power politics and resource competition without also understanding human behaviour and what exacerbates the fight undermines our effectiveness in preventing war and making peace.

Politics and international conflict is usually examined through the lens of *realpolitik*. *Realpolitik* is primarily about power: the rational evaluation and realistic assessment of the options available to one's own group and to an opposing one. This paradigm is a chess game of power relationships and the desire of elite groups to shape the world according to their own best interests. These dynamics operate in the world of economic and military calculations, strategic options, and political alliances and alignments. But conflict is more likely to be resolved if the geopolitical complexity is also placed in a context of human relationships. An experience of humiliation and powerlessness creates conditions in which groups are more likely to resort to violence. Respect, treating people with dignity, and inclusive politics that give groups and communities access to resources and influence over their lives are likely to forestall the advent of destructive behaviour.

My own training had helped me to understand the human mind and group behaviour, but what increasingly fascinated me was its relevance to the political process, particularly in areas of international conflict. Of course the link between experience and emotion, between pain and violence, between aggression and self-abuse is enormously relevant, and it is as crucial to an understanding of the behaviour of communities, ethnic groups, and nations as it is to understanding individuals. Yet this approach seemed to be almost completely ignored in the conventional approach to the analysis of conflicts, its causes, and the ways to resolve it. Writing this book provided the perfect opportunity to explore the link between politics and the human mind.

When asked to write this book, initially I was ambivalent, as I had never been an obvious admirer of Sigmund Freud's work. For me, he was too culture-bound, and he had created a theory that meant that practitioners were looking for certain aspects of human behaviour and then identifying them. It risks being an ideological position that makes all kinds of assumptions about human behaviour, as opposed to very careful listening and understanding as to why individuals and groups think and act in ways that are often unpalatable and difficult to digest. In psychotherapy, we need to start where people are, not where we want them to be. This is equally true of politics: we have a natural propensity to describe events through our own lens while omitting to understand the context, the history, and the nuances of culture, politics, and geography.

But Freud was also a genius. He made a very important contribution to understanding the human mind and issues of war and peace. For this reason, I became deeply immersed and stimulated in writing this book. He was profoundly original and one of the first powerful voices that recognised the power of the human mind to determine and shape events. Sadly, his insights are not dominant in the political arena. In the grand scheme of international politics, authority is shaped not by psychological understanding but by *realpolitik* and the use of power. International relations are seldom understood through the lens of people, human motivation, and what drives groups to behave in particular ways.

Some would argue that we will never fully prevent the emergence of such groups as Islamic State unless we do a full-frontal lobotomy on the human mind. Freud's belief that violence is part of the human condition is commonly shared.

According to Thomas Hobbes (1651), man in nature was naturally violent, and life was "nasty, brutish and short". He believed that man was driven by competition, rivalry, and the need for glory and would always wish to subdue the other. In his view, humans were programmed for socially organised violence; society had to be managed in such a way as to restrain them.

"The misanthropic Hobbesian view has prevailed because the impact of war in history makes war salient: like mountain peaks in a landscape wars are more visible than decades of peace" (Grayling, 2017, p. 126). The philosopher A. C. Grayling, in *War: An Enquiry* (2017), argues that the culturally dominant view about human behaviour is essentially pessimistic, where selfishness, greed, cruelty, and aggression are the drivers that increase the likelihood of going to war. Compare this idea with a more cultural view of war in which the impulse to go to war is not a genetic phenomenon but in the realm of human choice. As the author of this book, I believe that people are capable simultaneously of great destruction and great compassion; this will be dependent not on man's aggressive instinct but on the social environments in which people live and how far their fears and insecurities are addressed.

Psychoanalytic theory also claims that we all have an inner life that profoundly shapes how we think and act. It is therefore not sufficient to improve the conditions of the external world: we still have to work on our inner lives, as it is within this territory that our ability to be destructive lies. Our inner emotions are not always benign and generous. We are capable of being hateful, jealous, and envious and of imposing humiliation and degradation on others. According to the psychoanalyst M. Fakhry Davids (2011), "fostering in-depth awareness of the dark side of human nature" is man's task if he or she is to embrace a deeper understanding of a culture of conflict. Being human involves managing the destructive aspects of our behaviour, including impulses such as retribution and the desire to make another suffer.

When Freud wrote

Sigmund Freud was born to a Jewish family in the tumultuous, progressive year of 1848.

> The tide of revolutions that swept through Europe and the radical reforms that followed them heralded a new epoch for the Jews. . . . The feudal system was abolished, and Austrian Jews were granted their full political and civil rights as a result of these upheavals. [Whitebook, 2017, pp. 18, 21]

Prior to these reforms, Jews in the Austrian Empire had to obtain permission from the authorities to reside in a particular town. It was a time when it was possible to be hopeful; the forces of change and enlightenment were creating an atmosphere in which there was a "movement of emancipation, serving to inspire a richer and more lucid self-knowledge in man" (Yovel, 1992, p. 136).

Over the course of three generations,

> Freud's family went from being parochial Eastern European Jews, living in the very constricted world of Galician Jewry on the eastern periphery of the Austrian Empire, to secularised Jews inhabiting Vienna, one of the most cosmopolitan capitals of Western Europe. [Whitebook, 2017, p. 17]

In spite of their comparative affluence and the change in living circumstances, Freud spent his earliest life in cramped living conditions, with virtually no privacy. He was therefore exposed to "many of the elemental facts of life (e.g., bodily functions, sexuality, marital discord, pregnancy, birth, illness, and death) before he had the capacity to assimilate the excitement, anxiety, and confusion that such experiences engender in a small child" (Whitebook, 2017, p. 32). Freud's early life may well have shaped his theories on sexuality, "the touchstone of his entire project", which was to set the foundations of his work (Whitebook, 2017, p. 268).

Many of Freud's seminal works were written in the early twentieth century. *The Interpretation of Dreams* was published in 1900 and *The Psychopathology of Everyday Life* in 1901. He wrote at the time of the horrors of the First World War and the Great Depression of the 1930s. In an essay written soon after the outbreak of the First World War, Freud expressed his disillusionment about human nature and the supreme institution of the civilised world, namely the state. He later witnessed the rise of Nazi Germany and anti-Semitism in Europe, which ultimately resulted in the deaths of 6 million Jews. Having fled Nazi persecution in Vienna in 1938, Freud came to London as a refugee; he died there a year later, in 1939.

Freud's view of human nature was dark, but with much justification. The democratic secular world of liberal democracy was at war with fascism within months of his death. He observed the bleakest aspects of human behaviour, both in the socio-political system and in the inner workings of the human mind. Freud said of war, "we cannot but feel that no event has ever destroyed so much that is precious in the common possessions of humanity, confused so many of the clearest intelligences, or so thoroughly debased what is highest" (Freud, 1915b, p. 61).

Today the mood is darkening

The mood is darkening today, with people within liberal democracies fearing the rise of authoritarian rule. For many, the world is moving too fast, with

> rapid globalisation represent[ing] the loss of boundaries and our experience of time and space is shaken . . . the developments in information and communication technologies, greater speed and ease of travel and the borderless capacity for destruction in the nuclear age, all of which both excite interest and threaten large-group identity. [Alderdice, 2010b, pp. 314–315]

For many, the world does seem a more dangerous place. The rise of Islamic State has shaken the Middle East and the international order as we know it. For many, the world seems more chaotic, violent, and frightening. And yet there is a paradox: although the world seems more unsafe, many have experienced an improvement in their living conditions.

At the time of the fall of the Berlin Wall, two fifths of humanity was living in extreme poverty, while now it is one in eight (Goldin & Kutarna, 2016). But it is not an equitable distribution of resources, and in spite of the increased wealth, the disparities are now much more visible and are creating more disturbance:

> the world has never seen a greater accumulation of wealth, or a more extensive escape from material deprivation . . . nearly half of the world's income growth between 1988 and 2011 was appropriated by the richest tenth of humanity and, even in rich countries, there is a growing life-expectancy gap between classes. [Mishra, 2017, p. 324]

This income inequality is causing "status anxiety", and "evidence shows that in the developed countries, mental illnesses were three times as common in societies where there were bigger income differences between rich and poor" (Wilkinson, 2006, p. 711). This means that "an American is likely to know three times as many people with depression or anxiety problems as someone from countries such as in Japan and or Germany, where inequality is not as extreme" (pp. 711–732).

In the field of education: "In just over a generation, 3 billion more literate brains have joined the human race. With a few tragic exceptions, a child born almost anywhere today can expect to grow up healthier, wealthier and smarter than at any other time in history" (Goldin & Kutarna, 2016). "The world seems more literate, interconnected, and prosperous than at any other time in history. Average well-being has risen, if not equitably; economic misery has been alleviated in even the poorest parts of India and China" (Mishra, 2017, p. 7). But it is a climate in which human beings are programmed to maximise their self-interest at the cost of community and belonging.

Steven Pinker, in *The Better Angels of Our Nature* (2011), is clear that we have seen a significant reduction in violence and are moving progressively towards more peaceful behaviour. He sees this as a continuing trend in the twenty-first century. He has carried out a historical and statistical analysis in which he argues that our inner destructive demons are now giving way to more cooperative and altruistic behaviour. Despite these statistics, anxiety seems to be increasing in modern society. In the Western world, this is expressed in "some of the highest rates of depression, schizophrenia, poor health, anxiety, and chronic loneliness in human history. As affluence and urbanisation rise in a society, rates of depression and suicide tend to go *up* rather than down" (Junger, 2016, p. 19). There are those who would argue that one of the causes is "a world so focused on mindless consumption and status acquisition, [that] the developed world's epidemic of anxiety and depression should come as no surprise. Anxiety and depression are at unprecedented levels worldwide and the numbers are growing" (Peeble, 2017). Something is going wrong, and Freud may have something to say to illuminate our thinking.

Freud's views on human behaviour

The founding father of psychoanalysis, Freud was to reveal ideas of the subconscious desires of human beings, driven by aggressive impulses and sexual appetites. He was at the forefront in identifying the role of sexuality as a potential weapon of war, both as the abuse of power and a means to control. "Men are not gentle creatures who want to be loved", as Freud wrote in *Civilization and Its Discontents* (1930a), discussing ideas as relevant today as then. He talked about creatures with aggressive instincts, and how we perpetually created an enemy within ourselves. He was concerned about what would happen to our civilisation if we were unable to address some of these fundamental issues. Dostoyevsky's wise words stand in contrast, and carry a more hopeful view as to how we will redeem ourselves, when he wrote: "Hell is the inability to love, only healed by re-establishing a connection with another human being" (Dostoyevsky, 1880). Of course, the debate as to whether we are currently destroying our civilisation or whether we have the emotional maturity to prevent this destruction is an important one. How far is the capacity to love and be loved a metaphor for creating a less destructive society?

Freud would construct a so-called model of the mind in which the repression of conflict – the refusal to acknowledge competing (inner) voices – was deemed to be a core problem of mankind (Philips, 2014a). His ground-breaking books and papers were the roadmap to the human mind. Here he explored and theorised about dreams, culture, childhood development, sexuality, and mental health. He was the father and mother of the talking cures. There is now much evidence to support that talking helps alleviate emotional symptoms and lessens anxiety. By unleashing the unconscious, it acts as a means for bringing to the surface repressed aspects of the human mind. Defence mechanisms are, according to Freud, psychological strategies brought into play by the unconscious mind to manipulate, deny, or distort reality to protect against feelings of anxiety and unacceptable impulses.

The most familiar psychological defence mechanisms described by Freud are repression, rationalisation, projection, and denial. These are employed to externalise the discomfort experienced as a result of our raw emotions. The purpose of analysis or therapy would be to reveal what lies beneath the defence structures and to find ways to engage with these emotions that would not be destructive but enhance communication. In contemporary culture this might involve finding an emotionally intelligent language in order to communicate. War-like language does not address the underlying causes of the conflict but uses the threat of force as the communication.

As part of this process, Freud was interested in the developments necessary for mankind to achieve greater maturity. For him, for children to mature they must relinquish their infantile, idealised images of the parental figures and come to terms with parents as flawed, complex figures, which create ambivalent feelings in us as adults. It is the management and containment of these feelings that leads to maturity; failure to do so leads only to huge disappointment and the search for alternative idealised figures. We might call this growing up, where the individual is no longer dependent on the parents, nor looks for an equivalent parental figure to provide guidance. A more mature state is where the mind is more able to make independent decisions. The search for this idealised father figure, as I describe in those who signed up to joining Islamic State, may be a reflection of inadequate fathering that has not allowed this maturational process.

... all roads lead to childhood

For Freud, adults' behaviour, their experiences, and how they are perceived are rooted in childhood. He placed sexuality and the child's relations with its parents at the heart of the concept of cure. He was always concerned with what had been repressed in the mind and what we could not bear to think about. He was interested in finding a language that could bring these memories to the surface and connect the experiences and memories of childhood with adult life. He was concerned with how trauma and repression later gave rise to emotional blocks in adult behaviour that restricted growth and development and at times created physical symptoms. His primary concern was that early distorted sexual and violent memories created later disturbances. For this reason, Freud was committed to bringing those memories of childhood to the surface. His abiding preoccupation was the castration complex: he thought that castration anxiety is the conscious or unconscious fear of losing all or part of the sex organ, or the function of it. This castration anxiety refers to the fear of having one's genitalia disfigured or removed as punishment for sexual desires as a child.

According to Freud (1954), when the infant male becomes aware of differences between male and female genitalia, he assumes that the female's penis has been removed, and he becomes anxious that his own penis will be cut off by his rival, the father figure, as punishment for desiring the mother figure. For some, this literal interpretation may seem rather fanciful, but notions of sexual potency as a metaphor for having agency and impact in the world may have some relevance. "Catastrophes would take many forms and would be given many names in the psychoanalysis he would invent – birth, sexuality, castration, the Oedipus complex, displacement, narcissism, mourning, the death-drive" (Philips, 2014a, p. 50). For Freud, these were all rooted in childhood and sexuality. He was to say, "I have found in my own case too, the phenomena of being in love with my mother and jealous of my father, and I now consider it a universal event in early childhood" (Breger, 2000, p. 207). Many would criticise him for this generalised assumption and his inability to see beyond his own cultural lens. Psychological ideas need to be understood in the context of culture, history, and the way of life of particular communities.

Freud has also been criticised for focusing on the father figure; the mother is largely absent from his work. But ideas about attachment, with the identification of the importance of early mother–child separation, had not yet been researched. Feminist psychoanalytic theory later challenged this and introduced the early mother–child relationship as fundamental to its investigation. Central to Freud's theory was that as "a small child, a son will already begin to develop a special affection for his mother, whom he regards as belonging to him; he begins to feel his father as a rival who disputes his sole possession" (Freud & Freud, 2001, p. 207).

But, according to Freud, it is in the end the father's attention that the child wants, and the woman is relegated to a marginal role. Freud believed a "boy needs a firmly defined paternal figure". His theory is predicated on the idea that as the baby moves to early childhood, the intense relationship between mother and child needs a firm boundary, which is put in place by the father, who exerts discipline. Of course, current theory would say that this discipline can be down to either the mother or the father. His psychological theory was that a small child would move through what he called the Oedipal phase, where the young boy would want to theoretically kill his father in order to marry his mother. Freud would have believed that if the Oedipal phase was not achieved, the child remained in a state of grandiosity without recognising the limitations of its own power. If we transpose this theory to young people who are attracted to more extremist groups, it is possible to speculate that the young person has not had a firm parental boundary. He is then more likely to go in search of a strict, firm father figure. An obvious example of this is Islamic State.

Freud lived in a world dominated by cultural patrimony, and this profoundly shaped his theories. In addition, psychoanalytic theory at the time was reluctant to integrate the wider social and political context and how these ideas, such as changing roles in the family and the wider societal politics, shaped peoples' internal psychic state. Freud has been legitimately criticised for the limitations of how he saw the world, given, even in his time, the rise of women's emancipation. The wave of feminism in the 1960s and 1970s attacked Freud for being one the foremost patriarchal ideologues. Today, "there is a broad consensus that many of Freud's ideas on femininity were not simply wrong but at times downright daft" (Whitebook, 2017, p. 422).

Today, contemporary society still values ideas of maleness, which has much to do with fighting, strength, and the assertion of power. While there are cultural streams that identify the more feminine aspects of male identity, described as tenderness, vulnerability, and nurturing, they are not the attributes that are respected in those in positions of power. The cultural universe today "has been reconfigured by feminism, fundamental alterations in family structures, and the sexual revolution . . . to confront 'the repudiation of femininity', both clinically and culturally, in a way that Freud, the nineteenth-century patriarch, could not" (Whitebook, 2017, p. 422). According to Joel Whitebook, "if men did not have to repudiate the feminine . . . – the tender, dependent, vulnerable, receptive, and nurturing – parts of themselves, their possibilities for a fulfilled life would also be greatly enhanced" (p. 454). More to the point, it might mean we were less likely to go to war.

To understand Freud's profound contribution requires an understanding of its limits. His theory does not sufficiently address the role of women, and his thinking is profoundly paternalistic, but he was a product of the times. Later theorists would recognise that the workings of the inner mind were not primarily shaped by our aggressive and sexual impulses, as Freud believed, but were also profoundly influenced by experiences in the family and the socio-political context. In practice, this means that when a baby is born, it is shaped by where it is born, by its experience in the family, and by the wider politics. Later theorists recognised the important interplay between social factors, the environment, and the development of the interior landscape of each individual. So, if we start with where we are born, a baby born in Gaza, North Korea, or North London will already inhabit a different world of beliefs, value systems, and identity. The lens through which it will see the world will be digested through its mother's milk and will become part of its DNA.

Later ideas on human behaviour

Following Freud in the analytic school were intellectual heavy-weights such as Melanie Klein, who extended and developed Sigmund Freud's understanding of the unconscious mind. Klein, living and writing in the dark times of fascist Europe and post–Second World War, believed that central to therapy was to bring to the surface the aggressive aspects of human nature and reveal them to the individual. In the act of self-revelation, they would become less destructive. For Kleinians, getting hold of the aggressive, destructive aspect of human behaviour brought about change. By analysing children's play, much as Freud had analysed dreams, she explored the uncharted territory of the mind of the infant. Klein's understanding of the child's deepest fears, and its defences against them, enabled her to make original theoretical contributions, and she showed how these primitive mental states impact on the adult. Her ground-breaking theories have been taken up and developed by later generations of psychoanalysts.

Klein observed that children's play was symbolic of the internal mind of the child and spoke for children in a way that language could not. The term *internal objects* is commonly used in Kleinian theory to denote an inner mental and emotional representation of an external figure. For Klein, our inner worlds are populated with these internal objects. She understood the destructiveness of envy and our need to understand this aspect of our inner world, if we are not to act out destructive impulses in the outside world. Klein believed that much of behaviour was driven by envy, and because it is socially unacceptable to recognise this, we learn to repress these thoughts. For her, it was the recognition and taking responsibility for these emotions that would elevate us into more mature, socially responsible individuals.

Later, D. W. Winnicott, the English paediatrician and psychoanalyst, went on to develop more relational theories, which focused on the early mother–child relationship and the child's development. He attached great importance to the child's "basic trust" in the mother, and such concepts as "good-enough mothering". These theories have relevance to the child's maturational process. Failure to establish these early bonds of trust and attachment can lead to mistrust and a lack of safety in the world. Without the necessary secure attachments, the child, as it moves into adolescence, is more at risk of identifying with more extreme ideological positions that fill an empty relational void.

Later psychoanalysts had a more optimistic vision of human behaviour and developed the school of intersubjective thinking. The intersubjective school of psychoanalysts challenged the traditional, or classical, psychoanalysis of the myth that the mind develops in isolation. They argued that the individual's psychic structure develops in the context of relationships in the family, among peers, and in the wider community. Freudian theory failed to understand human behaviour and motivation as being shaped by our relationships. Atwood and Stolorow (2014) were the founding fathers of the intersubjective approach and believed that Freudian theory failed to understand how relationships shaped human behaviour. They believed that the way in which the individual evolved can only be understood in the light of their intersubjective relationships. This means that human behaviour is not primarily driven by innate impulses such as aggression, as Freud believed, but is dependent on the individual's interaction with the environment.

This development in psychoanalytic thinking was hugely important and could potentially link with how we think about war. If we believe that man is essentially aggressive, we will collude with the idea that war is inevitable. If we believe that war arises from the conditions that we create, the nature of political system, and the way people are treated, then this can reduce the possibilities of war. We can therefore hypothesise that if we put more human resources into creating just and equal societies where there is a deep understanding about human behaviour, then there is a likelihood that we will reduce the possibility of war.

TWO

Can war be avoided?

> History tells us that it is easier to get into a conflict than to get out; war and its consequences have their dangerous algorithms, feeding on themselves with a devastating momentum of their own. The road to war may look like a careful strategic assessment; more likely it is mired in a deep fog of misunderstanding and misreading which can unleash an unpredictable chain of events, with governments going to war with little understanding of the consequences.
>
> Rifkind & Picco, 2014, p. 157

In July 1932, Albert Einstein asked Freud, "Is there any way of delivering mankind from the menace of war?" (Einstein & Freud, 1933). Freud replied that "the growth of emotional ties between men must operate against war" and concluded that "whatever makes for cultural development is working also against war". Full of insight, Freud was to describe how man loses his capacity for rational thought once engaged in war:

> Science herself has lost her passionless impartiality . . . the anthropologist is driven to declare the opponent inferior and

> degenerate; the psychiatrist to publish his diagnosis of the enemy's disease of mind or spirit . . . [the] sense of these immediate evils is disproportionately strong. [Freud, 1947, p. 245]

Writing "Thoughts for the Times on War and Death" (1915b), Freud's voice is that of the bewildered civilian, looking on as their country is preparing to take up arms against fellow citizens of Europe. While he is disturbed, he is sanguine and considers people's sense of shock to be unjustified, as what they are experiencing is the destruction of an illusion. For Freud, this illusion is the belief that the conduct of leaders and individuals of civilised nations will be guided by high moral standards.

In the *Why War* correspondence between Einstein and Freud (1933), Einstein turns to Freud because he is aware that there are "strong psychological factors at work" that paralyse the good intentions of organisations such as the League of Nations. Freud agrees that a supra-national peace-keeping agency would be effective only if endowed with the necessary power. He points out that the League of Nations fails because its authority relies solely on an appeal to certain idealistic attitudes. Law, he notes, "was originally brute violence and even today it cannot do without the support of violence". He is not very optimistic about mankind's ability to work together for the greater good and believes that human greed and desire for power makes individuals self-serving and incapable of finer ideals.

War creates in ordinary people the capacity to be hugely destructive, but – Freud said – man can "very inadequately be classified as 'good' or 'bad'. A human being is seldom altogether good or bad; he is usually 'good' in one relation and 'bad' in another . . .", war creates the conditions where the worst aspects of human nature are amplified (Freud, 1947, p. 245). According to Sebastian Junger, who has done a great deal of research on war and why people fight, "the core psychological experiences of war are so primal and unadulterated . . . that they eclipse subtler feelings, like sorrow or remorse, that can gut you quietly for years" (Junger, 2011, p. 145). "There is a tipping point in armed conflict when the fight for survival stimulates the kind of aggression that magnifies hatred and perpetuates the most destructive aspects of human behavior" (Rifkind, Picco, & Wilson, 2014, p. 1).

The psychological value of going to war

It was Freud's treatment of soldiers during the war that helped him to develop his insights into human behaviour and its motivations. He was to write that war neuroses took place not when the soldier was in danger, but, rather, when the soldier was himself the *cause* of such danger. The soldier is taught that cruelty is not wrong in itself, but only when done towards the wrong person at the wrong time. What Freud is saying is that it is the soldier's internal conflict about war and killing that is the cause of the soldier's troubled state of mind. David Grossman, a psychologist and soldier, observed that there was "a powerful innate resistance towards killing one's own species which armies had to work hard to develop psychological mechanisms to overcome; and the acts of overcoming this resistance was one of the primary causes of trauma" (Grossman, 1996, p. xxxix).

Freud identified how war unleashes the cruellest, most barbaric aspects of human behaviour, which are kept hidden in ordinary civilised interactions.

All sorts of previously forbidden and buried impulses, cruel, sadistic, murderous and so on, are stirred to greater activity . . .

the aggressive acts for which the soldier must be hourly prepared, for besides the readiness to die, the readiness to kill is
demanded of him. [Lomas, 2000, p. 236]

If the soldier can convince himself of the rightness of the cause
for which he is fighting and that he is protecting his country
and his family, he is less likely to be less conflicted. In the First
World War, soldiers saw combatants of all nations trapped
in an insoluble deadlock in the trenches marked by "years of
slow, methodical battlefield encounters danced to the music
of butchery" and a period of "senseless slaughter with front-
line tales, the squalor, and suicidal bravery, the culling of the
youngest and best that has stuck in people's minds" (Ralston,
1992, p. 198; see also Marr, 2009, p. 118). When the soldier
can no longer believe in his actions, he finds himself in a state
of mental conflict, and this is what would have brought the
soldier to Freud's consulting room.

Like other writers, Freud recognised that war could be
exhilarating; the camaraderie of war conditions is often
remembered fondly. War has the power to inflict terrible
psychological harm on those in its path, but at the same time
it forges strong bonds within communities aligned against a
common enemy. This is beneficial for the human sense of con-
nectedness and belonging and is unparalleled in modern culture. Émile Durkheim, a French sociologist and philosopher,
found that when European countries went to war, suicide
rates dropped. In Paris, the psychiatric wards were surpris-
ingly empty during both World Wars. Sebastian Junger has
some interesting reflections on the subject. "When people are
actively engaged in a cause their lives have more purpose . . .
with a resulting improvement in mental health . . . people will
feel better psychologically if they have more involvement with
their community" (Junger, 2016, p. 49).

According to Charles Fritz's, "Disaster" (1961), modern society has been gravely disrupted, and, consequently, so too have the social bonds that bind us together. Disasters, he argues, create a community of sufferers that allows individuals to experience an immensely reassuring connection to others. This contemporary alienation may also be part of the reason why young men and women in search of meaning and the desire to feel a community may find themselves drawn to such groups as Islamic State. It is this sense of belonging and feeling part of a large group that is so powerful. Junger writes that "war also inspires ancient human virtues of courage, loyalty, and selflessness [which is] utterly intoxicating to the people who experience them . . . [this] demonstrates war's ability to ennoble people rather than just debase them" (Junger, 2016, p. 77). In war, "class differences are temporarily erased, income disparities become irrelevant, race is overlooked, and individuals are assessed simply by what they are willing to do for the group" (p. 54). Our fundamental desire is to belong and feel connected to other human beings. War can serve this function.

Nature of war

Freud (1915b) accurately identified the increased dangers of war that arose from the use of more sophisticated weaponry. He stated that "the war in which we had refused to believe broke out . . . more sanguinary and more destructive than any other war of other days, because of the enormously increased perfection of weapons of attack and defence" (Freud, 1915b, pp. 289–293). How right he was, and our intense focus on terrorism has helped to spawn a veritable counterterrorism industrial military complex, made up of new government agencies, private firms, and an army of well-funded advisers who are highly motivated to keep the issue high on the national agenda. Governments are now putting huge resources into armaments, military intelligence, targeting, logistics, force protection, and allied coordination (Livesey, 2015). While these are necessary activities, surveillance and security do not engage with human solutions and what they might look like. It does not address why people behave in particular ways, what makes them become a threat, and what makes them angry and alienated – and, more to the point, what would make them behave differently.

According to Rob Malley, who was a senior advisor on terrorism to President Obama, our response to terrorism will need to be more proportionate. The aim of terrorism is to frighten ordinary citizens, and with the help of governments they are succeeding. Of course, the global terrorist threat requires a serious and sober analysis and response. But

> political expediency, and fear has become divorced from facts, with profound impact on domestic politics. . . . . In the years after 2001, an average of fewer than nine Americans per year have been killed in terror attacks on American soil, compared, for example, with an average of about 12,000 a year who are shot to death in non-terror related incidents. President Barack Obama was ridiculed for noting (correctly) that more Americans die each year falling in the bathtub than from terrorism. [Finer & Malley, 2017]

The resources committed to military hardware are a demonstration of our wealth but not our humanity. In this ever-militarised society, "every misdirected bomb, every brutal night raid, every non-combatant killed, every lie and denial and minimisation becomes a recruitment poster for those at war with the US" (Monbiot, 2015). While we rightly label Islamic State a terrorist group, we do not consider the fact that

> air strikes are a form of terror. Even if they are very precise and there is no collateral damage, air strikes are terrifying; they destroy buildings and create fear. Even if targeting is precise, the intelligence on which targets are located is prone to error so that innocent people are bound to be killed. [Kaldor & Turkmani, 2015]

The nature of warfare has changed, and yet there has not been a sophisticated debate as to whether our commitment to military solutions is making the world more or less safe. One of the lessons of the Second World War was that weakness was a dangerous response to the threat of force, and those marshalling the greatest military power would ultimately win the war. Our current experience challenges this old logic, as most wars are no longer between states, but within states. The use of force over the past two decades has brought greater chaos to the world. It can be argued that this, along with other contributing factors, has unleashed a powerful asymmetrical backlash in the form of violent jihadi extremism.

It is war that creates the conditions where communities, who had previously lived happily together, resort to more polarised and adversarial identities. In Iraq, Sunni and Shia had, for the most part, coexisted throughout their history, with very few periods of sectarian violence. During the civil war that was catalysed by the Anglo–American invasion of Iraq in 2003, the brutality was limitless. Those who had previously lived harmoniously became trapped in hatred and the desire for retribution. A kind of insanity emerged. In Samar Yazbek's very powerful book, *The Crossing: My Journey to the Shattered Heart of Syria*, she talks about how people no longer feel human, describing how they feel like animals, and where their drives are morphed into kill or be killed (Yazbek, Gowanlock, & Ahmedzai Kemp, 2016). Moral clarity is comforting for all of us, with indicators of good and bad behaviour – but in war everybody is behaving badly. There is little to suggest clean war on one side; in conflict, all sides regress and do enormous harm to each other.

Terrorism

The definition of war is armed conflict between states or nations, or between identifiable and organised groups within a state – the latter being the definition of civil war. Asymmetric warfare is one between unequal combatants. In an asymmetric war, often between the state and non-state actors, the state has access to sophisticated weapons; the non-state actor, often in the form of terrorist groups, would have no access to war planes or tanks or sophisticated and costly weapons. They would therefore devise ways to create maximum disturbance and create a backlash using methods that disturb the population, such as suicide bombs, roadside bombs, and attacks on industrial installations. In Iraq, non-state actors were later to use roadside bombs, which were comparatively cheap, low-risk, and didn't get civilians killed.

In practice, terrorism and jihad have existed for many years; they go back at least as far as the anarchist movement of the late nineteenth century. This form of "globalised terror" is expressed by choosing symbolic locations where innocent civilians are targeted, with no regard for national borders. The twentieth century has witnessed the most egregious examples of state terror, with the horrors of the Holocaust, Stalin's purges, and the killing fields of the Pol Pot regime. Today, most examples of terrorism are non-state actors who do not have the sophisticated weapons of the state; their activity can be described as "acts that attempt to disrupt, overthrow, or simply express rage against the existing political order" (Volkan, 1998, p. 156). It can certainly be argued that war is a creator of terrorism where the side with less power and without the weapon of the state devises methods to disturb and create chaos for the enemy. "A terrorist is someone who has a bomb but doesn't have an air force" (Martinez, 2016, p. 123). Today Islamic State is an example of this.

Scott Atran, an anthropologist at the University of Michigan, has made a close study of the psychological and social motivations behind jihadism; he argues that Islamic State is really no different from the "revolutionary-romantic movements that have revelled in bloodshed throughout history" (Atran, 2015b). If this is so, then the alarmist response from the West to the group's brutality may have fuelled its growth. "Western sensationalism has perversely contributed to the lure and glamour of ISIS as much as it has to its lurid appeal to the young and disaffected" (Weiss & Hassan, 2015, p. 129).

This is not the first time that we have seen the rise of such destructive groups in our society. Perhaps most revealing is the recognition that this form of terrorism has much to do with a sense of "anomie", of being lost and alienated from communities. "Violent extremism represents not the resurgence of traditional cultures, but their collapse, as young people unmoored from millennial traditions flail about in search of a social identity that gives personal significance and glory" (Atran, 2015b). The search for identity becomes a key part of this, as the dark side of globalisation robs individuals of a clear sense of identity and belonging. In this new reality, "vertical lines of communication between the generations are replaced by horizontal peer-to-peer attachments that can cut across the globe" (Atran, 2015b).

What creates conditions for evil?

Freud was writing at one of the darkest times in history. He witnessed the rise of fascism and saw, in the rise of Nazi Germany, some of the most disturbing signs of man's capacity to be evil. Islamic State has been called evil; we need, therefore, to ask the question of what we mean by evil and where we think it comes from. Much has been written about the nature of evil and the conditions in which societies break down, where there is no protection against the most destructive aspects of human behaviour. The political theorist Hannah Arendt, a Jewish woman who escaped Nazi Germany, observed: "The sad truth is that most evil is done by people who never make up their minds to be or do either evil or good" (Arendt, 1978, p. 180). Arendt took the position that there can be "lesser evils". It came to define how well-meaning citizens might be made to collaborate with totalitarian regimes. For her, it explained how so many Germans participated in the horrors of the Holocaust, horrors that could only have been executed on such a massive scale if a large number of people obeyed orders (Arendt, 1978). Benjamin Ferencz was the chief prosecutor at the Nuremberg Trials, and he has spent his life trying to deter war and war crimes. Legendary in the world of international law, he never stops pushing his message: "War makes murderers out of otherwise decent people, all wars, and all decent people" (in Stahl, 2017). Referring to the Nazi higher echelons of power, whom he prosecuted at Nuremberg, he was to reply, when asked at interview whether those who perpetrated war crimes would otherwise have been normal, upstanding citizens: "These men would never have been murderers had it not been for the war. . . . These were people who could quote Goethe, who loved Wagner, who were polite" (in Stahl, 2017).

Bernard-Henri Levy, the French philosopher, takes a different position: "It was better to agree on evil than on good, and once we agreed on what is evil, it is the role of politics to figure out how to lessen it" (Levy, 2008, p. 70). He argues that it is necessary to work out what makes the world a little more liveable for the greatest number of people, and that we should not, therefore, make concessions about human rights. For him, since evil seems to be lurking behind every attempt at political transformation and any liberation struggle, "the destiny of the West was to fight that evil whose traces could be found, paradoxically, in any project predicated on an articulation of the idea of the totalitarian or egalitarian good" (in Weizman, 2011, p. 38).

In the atmosphere of the 1930s, Germany became entrenched in a climate of bitter anger following the humiliation of the Treaty of Versailles and the mass unemployment and poverty that resulted from the global market crash of 1929. Furious with the Weimar government for its perceived weakness and inability to protect its people, much of German civil society became convinced of the need for strong leadership. In combination with an exceptional anti-minority propaganda campaign, this environment lent itself to a protectionist mindset and the hunt for someone to apportion blame to. The Nazis offered themselves as the only answer to the wrongdoing and ignominy of post–World War One humiliation.

Classic obedience studies by Stanley Milgram and Philip Zimbardo later revealed that, under certain conditions, ordinary people easily slip into roles where they unquestioningly carry out violence against others, if only because instructed to do so by an authority figure (Milgram, 1963, p. 371; Haney, Banks, & Zimbardo, 1973). In Nazi Germany, where disobedience could be punished with death and minority hatred was the norm, there was no room for diverging opinions, and the rigid ideology of Nazism was set. Arendt argued that once inducted into the hierarchical structure of an army, a man or woman becomes an instrument to be wielded by their superiors, and it is at that moment that benevolent individuals can be turned into killing machines. She was to argue that the worst crimes – war, genocide, slavery, and the subjugation of women – are made possible by mechanisms of control that induce obedience on a mass scale.

The philosopher Peter Singer (1981) uses the term "moral circle" to describe how we place some beings in a privileged category, worthy of our full moral concern, and others outside it. Research into moral exclusion suggests that to humanise and privilege "in-groups" while dehumanising "out-groups" is a ubiquitous phenomenon (Opotow, 1990). Former Chief Rabbi Jonathan Sacks (2015) wisely observes how we are naturally inclined to favour members of our in-group and fear the members of other groups. He comments that this results in behaviour where the greater the threat from the outside, the stronger the sense of cohesion within.

> At the heart of a relationship based on obedience is an imbalance of power. . . . What makes us free is not the power to choose, but the power to turn our choices into expressions of our own values. We expand our freedom when we transform the power to choose into the power to create, when we identify the things that matter to us and dedicate ourselves to them. This is "creative freedom". [Martinez, 2016, p. 216]

There is a common shorthand to describe Islamic State as evil, but the depressing reality is the ordinariness of the young men and women who join this organisation. In a 2017 public lecture, Clarissa Ward, a CNN journalist, tells the story of a young man, Mohammad. In her lecture, Ward says of Islamic

State, "they aren't evil psychopaths. People reach a breaking point, they feel they have no other option left" (2017). These are her words:

> This young man, Mohammad, loved Keats and poetry; he was dreaming of what he wanted to do. The family had no money but gave everything to take care of their guests and displayed incredibly hospitality. One day, Mohammad left the family home to cover a demonstration for a news report and as he travelled back he saw bombs falling on his village, attached to parachutes which allowed the planes to clear out of the blast zone. When he returned to his own house a bomb had landed next door, killing his neighbour, a young woman, and an 8-year-old child. The house had been demolished. Mohammad tried to calm people and help extract bodies next door. His traumatised sister spent the night rocking back and forth on the floor in the foetal position, wailing "planes, planes." Over the next year, he and his family continued living in a state of abject fear. He could do nothing to materially provide for his family. The family was unable to leave as they were too poor, so life continued getting more and more despairing. There was the chemical attack in Damascus where 1,300 were killed. Mohammad and his community felt intense bitterness, as they had been abandoned in their experience. He realized there was going to be no external protection and slumped into a deep depression. He stopped responding to messages on Skype. A year later, his family finally got a message back from him saying he was in Raqqa. This did not make sense: Mohammad was not the kind of person who would fight, especially not with ISIS. After many unacknowledged messages in which I asked what had happened – this was not who he was – I finally received a response. He replied "you don't know Mohammad so good any more". [Ward, 2017]

THREE

Religion: the search for a powerful father?

Freud's essential thesis was that religion is a man-made construct for protection from the painful vicissitudes of life. Whether it be fundamentalist or mainstream, he felt it to be an expression of unresolved individual, psychological issues from childhood. This is referred to as *"theodicy* – that is, the attempt to provide a rationale for the ultimate meaningless-ness of human existence as well as for the inexorability and ubiquity of human suffering" (Whitebook, 2017, p. 403). According to Freud, the terrifying impression of helplessness in childhood arouses the need for protection, which could be provided through the love of a father. He believed that religion was rooted in the search for a powerful father and concluded that

> the search for God was to seek an omnipotent father, an image of God, to assuage the feeling of vulnerability; thus, religion is related to shared illusion. . . . "God created man in his own image", as "Man created God in his". [Freud, 1927c, pp. 19–20]

According to Whitebook, other thinkers, such as Émile Durkheim, argued that the religious impulse, like sexuality and aggression, is a permanent feature of human reality that every conceivable human society must find a way to accommodate. It is therefore incumbent on a proponent of secularisation like Freud to propose possible functional equivalents for religion, as Durkheim called them, in a post-religious society. [Whitebook, 2017, p. 403]

Freud never pursued the question of what post-religious alternatives could be available to those who were disillusioned. Freud himself was famously a "Godless Jew". He was a committed liberal, rationalist, and champion of the Enlightenment and was intellectually committed to social progress through science, education, and liberal politics.

Even today, psychoanalysts continue to interpret religious practice as the redirection of immature impulses into mature and socially acceptable conduct. "The psychoanalytic understanding of belief-system formation also changed" (Volkan, 2014, p. 127). British psychoanalyst D. W. Winnicott's description of what he called *transitional objects* enlarged psychoanalytic theory concerning the foundation of religious beliefs and feelings (Volkan, 2014, p. 127). Winnicott argued that during early development, a child learning to accept the external reality of objects must place objects outside its control, creating an "intermediate area of experience". The transitional object occupies a place between inner and outer reality, thereby aiding in the child's transition from its inner world to the world outside. Winnicott supposed that this object represents the union between mother and infant, easing the loss of the mother's breast and the anxieties of coming into a harsh reality. Religion, in Winnicott's view, is one such transitional phenomenon, operating in the intermediate space between inner and outer reality.

Religion is not a "universal neurosis", as Freud thought; it is much more multifaceted in its meaning. Religion can serve the function of replacing a personal sense of helplessness, shame, and humiliation with religious identification with the large-group identity. French sociologist Gustave Le Bon "postulated that an individual within a group loses much of his distinctiveness and acts instead in accordance with the homogenous urges that unite the group" (Kogan, 2007, p. 72). Religion has the capacity to demonstrate great love and tolerance, but it can also be ideological. There is, of course, a long history of people fighting wars in the name of religion. But according to Jonathan Sacks (2015), it is not religion itself that is the source of violence, but human behaviour. Sacks references Hobbes (1651) and his belief that man is driven by competition, rivalry, and the need for glory and would always wish to subdue the other.

Today we see a deep polarisation between religious and secular life, with an increased intolerance of the choices made by others. Those of secular belief attack monotheistic religions for believing they have the monopoly on truth, whereas

> those of religious faith often believe that secularists have lost their moral compass. Although the twentieth century has taught us that no doctrine has the monopoly on human values, whether we are talking about communism, liberalism, nationalism or religious values, all seem to fail when trying to improve the quality of the majority of people's lives (Rifkind & Picco, 2014, p. 95).

Religion has often served as a moral frame to help manage lives that were painful and unrewarding. It has offered a sense of community and a feeling of belonging and protection in an unsafe world. Throughout history, most religions have encouraged people to reflect on themselves and to control their darker impulses to behave destructively. But this is not a natural state, and our tendency is to avoid self-reflection, to see the world through our own eyes, to think that our thought processes are superior to others'. We have little insight into our own motivation. Our limited capacity for self-reflection restricts our ability to recognise our own motivation and, in extension, our impact upon others. Similarly, those who joined up to Islamic State may well be an exaggerated version of these "action–oriented individuals who characteristically spent little time in introspection. Their response to any environmental threat was to engage in a furor of activity which rapidly dissipated the developing tension" (Atran, 2015b).

The history of Islam

Islam, the last of the Abrahamic faiths following Judaism and Christianity, emerged in the seventh century in the Arabian Peninsula. At the time, Muhammad was believed to be the last in line of God's messengers, who received the oral revelation of the Quran over a period of twenty-three years. Islam has now existed for more than 1,400 years and today has more than one and a half billion followers.

> 85 percent of all Muslims are Sunni; the remaining 15 percent are Shi'i or Sufi. . . . Although Islam finds its origins in the Arabian Peninsula, the overwhelming majority of Muslims are not Arab. The largest Muslim countries – including Indonesia, Bangladesh, and Pakistan – are not part of the Middle East. [Hidayatullah, 2003, pp. 257, 259]

The last caliphate was the Ottoman empire, which was in its ascendancy until the sixteenth century and then experienced a gradual decline, until Mustafa Kemal Atatürk, the founder of the Republic of Turkey, euthanised it in 1924.

For over a century, Sunni Islam has been grappling with its loss of status as the region's traditional ruling sect. It watched, at times passively, as minorities took power and carved Sunni Islam's heartland into Israel, Lebanon, Syria, and then Iraq. [Hidayatullah, 2003, p. 259]

The phenomenon known today as political Islam has only existed for a century. The more extreme version of Islam has been shaped and influenced by Wahhabi thought.

How Islamic State emerged out of a Wahhabi philosophy

By 1790, the foundations of Wahhabi thought were present across the entire Persian Gulf region. Adherents spread fear and obedience throughout the Arabian Desert, using brutal punishment such as the severing of feet, hands, and heads. There was an eighteenth-century mutual aid pact between Ibn Saud and Ibn Abd al-Wahhab: under the terms of this power-sharing arrangement with the Wahhabi clerics, the political legitimacy of the House of Saud was guaranteed. "In return the royal family continues to refrain from a basic interference with the ultra-puritanical Sunni foundations of the country" (Aarts & Roelants, 2015, p. 15). This mutual self-serving agreement is still in existence today, and it restricts reforming aspirations of the Saudi government, who are straightjacketed by the conservative traditions of the Wahhabis. But the pact plays its part in protecting and reinforcing the survival of the regime.

Under Wahhabi influence, the Kingdom of Saudi Arabia has been marketing its own vision of Islam for years. This oil-rich country has financed 210 Islamic centres around the world, as well as 1,500 mosques, 202 Islamic faculties, and 2,000 schools, all of them filled with Wahhabi scholars and books propagating Saudi teachings. Their influence reaches deep into Bosnia, Chechnya, London, Canada, and the United States. These religious schools were supposed to protect Muslims from Western influence and lead them back to a strict, purist Islam.

The crux of Wahhabi thought is that only Allah is to be worshipped, and therefore Jews, Christians, Shia, and Alawites were excommunicated. Saudi Wahhabism is a particularly harsh form of Salafism. Jihadist Salafism is a combination of Qutb's violent theory of revolution – in which it was through violence that change came about – and Wahhabi religious doctrine. For Wahhabis, it is not just about a return to the Islam of the "pious forefathers", but also about enmity towards every form of unbeliever.

The beginnings of Islamic State

Islamic State is deeply influenced by Wahhabi ideology. Its leader, Abu Omar al-Baghdadi, who became emir of the Islamic State of Iraq in 2006, holds a PhD in Quranic Studies. Religious dogma has been a hallmark of al-Baghdadi's life from the beginning; he has spent much of his time devotedly practicing oratory and religious instruction. As a child, al-Baghdadi was quiet and reserved but prone to fits of anger, particularly directed at those whom he considered to be engaging in "un-Islamic" behaviour. He would become animated while leading other children in reciting Quranic scripture at the mosque where his father taught. Several of his family members – including possibly his father – are believed to have been adherents of Salafi Islam but were also members of the Baathist party.

Under Saddam Hussein's Faith Campaign, in which tens of thousands of new jobs teaching Quranic scripture were created, al-Baghdadi's family connections helped him win a position to study for his doctorate at the Saddam University for Islamic Studies. During this time, at his uncle's suggestion, al-Baghdadi joined the Muslim Brotherhood, where he gravitated towards a radical group of Salafist jihadis. This included his older brother Jum'a and his mentor Muhammad Hardan, who had fought in the war against the Soviets in Afghanistan in the 1980s.

In 2004, al-Baghdadi was arrested while visiting a friend who was on the American terrorist watch list, and he was sent to Camp Bucca in Iraq. Unbeknownst to his American jailors, who classified him as a civilian inmate, al-Baghdadi had already helped to found the insurgent group Jaysh Ahl al-Sunna wa-l-Jamaah [Army of the People of the Sunna and Communal Solidarity], which fought against the United States in northern and central Iraq during the occupation. At Camp Bucca, al-Baghdadi established networks of control between groups of prisoners, beginning to assert himself as a dominant and charismatic leader, aiding in the indoctrination of new inmates, and building the foundations for the future of Islamic State.

At the time, the world paid little attention to his rise. The catastrophic war in Iraq, with the murder and displacement of millions of Iraqis, came after a decade of sanctions and embargoes (Mishra, 2015). The dismantling of the Iraqi army, de-Baathification, and the Shia domination after the war provoked the formation in Mesopotamia of al-Qaeda, the precursor to Islamic State (Mishra, 2015). This made the ground fertile for the rise of Islamic State, reflecting the terrible political vacuum in the region. "For many, the grievances that generated the Arab uprisings have not been addressed. Unemployment and thwarted aspirations remain their lot" (Hollis, 2015). The popularity of Islamic State was further fuelled by the fact that the quotient of frustration tends to be highest in countries that have a large population of educated young men who have undergone multiple shocks and displacements in their transition to modernity and yet find themselves unable to fulfil the promise of self-empowerment (Mishra, 2015).

"IS propaganda promises social welfare, a fulfilling family life, and an end to the march of Western cultural decadence and materialism" (Hollis, 2015).

> IS offers a postmodern collage rather than a coherent doctrine. Born from the ruins of two nation states that dissolved in sectarian violence, it is a beneficiary . . . of the failure of governments to fulfil their basic roles: to create or maintain a stable political order, protect their citizens from external turbulence. [Mishra, 2017, p. 89]

And despite the poisonous ideology that has emerged, many people felt safer under the harsh rule of Islamic State than in the chaos of the war in the region and the experience of being displaced. Some citizens from Turkish refugee camps choose to return because life under Islamic State offers greater protection.

The chaos of war leaves a terrible political vacuum in which citizens feel unprotected. Hardline political groups, such as the Taliban or even Islamic State, are initially welcomed by some, as they create order. The nature of the justice is harsh, but there is some relief among local populations as it creates a degree of order amidst the chaos.

> Much of the early support for Islamic State came from the battered and frightened Sunni communities of eastern Syria and western Iraq dependent on the group's ability to provide

security justices and services. Now that Islamic State can no longer act as a government, the inhabitants are more likely to turn against their brutal rulers. [Burke, 2017]

The romance with Islamic State did not last long, as its aim is to stimulate sectarian violence and draw people into their rigid and savage ideology, which imposes a draconian order, enforcing beheadings, stoning of adulterers, and amputations. An example of its brutality was its treatment of the Yazidis, which marked a new height of brutality and bloodshed. Men and women were massacred and dumped in shallow graves, and Islamic State fighters legitimated a system of sexual slavery where they claimed that the rape of non-Muslim women was a form of worship.

Insurgent organisations understand and exploit the need for justice and order. Islamic State imposes their rule of law in a dictatorial and hardline manner. It is no surprise that al-Shabaab's predecessor was the Islamic Courts Union. The genesis of the Taliban, too, was couched in a justice response to corruption. These insurgent groups find success in their imposition of a sense of justice. Human rights are perceived as a relationship between citizen and state, and when the state fails to protect its citizens – or causes profound suffering – the sense of injustice felt by communities is exploited by insurgencies to impose their will and own version of the law.

In the early days of the establishment of Islamic State, Abu Omar al-Baghdadi started recruiting ex-Baathists from Saddam Hussein's army. Although

previously seen as secular Sunnis, these officers were willing to grow their beards and take on an Islamic character to blend in with al-Baghdadi's forces. All of them had been collectively discharged from the Iraqi army with no pension when Paul Bremer, President George W. Bush's envoy to Iraq and the practical ruler of the country at the time, disbanded the Iraqi army after the fall of Baghdad in 2003. [Moubayed, 2015, p. 104]

From Saddam Hussein's example, al-Baghdadi learned persistence and brutality. Saddam Hussein was the Iraqi alpha male: cruel, unforgiving, and uncompromising. [p. 100]

These ex-Baathist officers were experienced soldiers who were well trained in war, communications, discipline and siege. [p. 112]

Sunni Arabs constitute at most 20 percent of Iraq's population, whereas Shia Arabs constitute as much as 65 percent. A plurality of Sunni Kurds (17 percent), plus smaller demographics of Christians, Assyrians, Yazidis, and Sunni and Shia Turkmen make up the fabric of the rest of the country's society. But Saddam had presided over decades of a sectarian patronage system that broadly favoured the minority at the expense of a much-impoverished and restive majority. [Weiss & Hassan, 2015, p. 25]

The rise of Islamic State was a backlash against the Shiite rule and domination in the new Iraq where Sunni representation was to be marginalised. The Sunni/Shiite balance was being recalibrated, with the rise of strong Shiite leaders in the regions, including the rising influence of Iranian Shiite, in part through the mentoring of Hezbollah leader Hasan Nasrallah of Hezbollah in Lebanon. What may be observed today is Sunni Muslims being where the Shia were thirty-five years ago: "they feel weak, leaderless, victimized and abandoned" (Moubayed, 2015, p. 20).

The Taliban's strategy is to undermine traditional social structures, replacing local leaders with more radical mullahs and swiftly installing Sharia law and courts to enforce and deliver swift and often brutal justice. They levy taxes and conscript fighters and labourers. They consistently support weaker, disenfranchised, or threatened tribes, claiming to protect Afghan and Islamic identity against the occupying infidel Christian crusaders. They recognise familiar and trusted structures based on and operating under traditional tribal customs, intended to convey an otherwise absent sense of security, fairness, and stability to the local people and thereby usurp the power and replace the authority of the weakened Afghan government at all levels. This foundation of control is based upon meeting the needs of local communities, and exploiting it as an "Islamic duty", by making provisions that the state cannot provide. In situations where a breakdown of law and order occurs, it is felt to be better to have a harsh provision of an ordered society than nothing.

Who is Islamic State?

It is easy to dismiss Islamic State as merely a collection of psychopaths. A proportion of Islamic State fighters, drawn from the Middle East and Europe, do fit the mould of disaffected, aggressive opportunists seeking an outlet for their most violent impulses. As Vamık Volkan (1998), who has conducted extensive research on the mindset of terrorists, points out, terrorist leaders are rarely mentally ill: many are highly intelligent, with the ability for strategic planning, even if personal identity problems are common among them. "Out of the range of possible responses to identity problems, terrorist leaders tend to shore up their internal sense of self by seeking the power to hurt and by expressing their sense of entitlement to power" (Volkan, 1998, p. 161).

It is too easy to dismiss the group as ill-educated in religious theology; this may be true of its recruits, particularly the foreign fighters, but in its higher ranks runs a strong thread of religious understanding. Graeme Wood highlights that "the religion preached by its most passionate followers derives from coherent and even learned interpretations of Islam. Its commitment is to return civilization to a seventh-century legal environment, and ultimately to bring about the apocalypse" (Wood, 2015).

In contrast to this, there are terrorist experts who claim that "what inspires the most lethal assailants today is not so much the Quran but a thrilling cause and a call to action that promises glory and esteem in the eyes of friends" (Atran, 2015b). Scott Atran writes,

> There is little recognition of its genuine appeal, and even less of the joy it engenders. The mainly young people who volunteer to fight for it unto death feel a joy that comes from joining with comrades in a glorious cause, as well as a joy that comes from satiation of anger and the gratification of revenge (whose sweetness, says science, can be experienced by brain and body much like other forms of happiness). [Atran, 2015b]

Lord Alderdice, a psychoanalyst who writes about terrorism and some of its destructive satisfactions, says

> it should not be forgotten that during violent conflicts there are gains for both individuals and groups which must then be relinquished in the cause of peace . . . who may have to settle for mundane jobs and lives . . . powerful, exciting, abusive positions that violence offers those involved officially or illegally in the use of force. [Alderdice, 2010a, p. 30]

Oliver Roy, one of the most interesting and sometimes provocative thinkers on Jihad, clearly distinguishes

> between the version of Islam espoused by IS which is much more grounded in the methodological tradition of exegesis of the prophet Muhammad's words, and ostensibly based on the

work of "scholars" – and the Islam of the Jihadis who claim allegiance to IS, which first of all revolves around a vision of heroism and modern-day violence. [Roy, 2017b]

In his most recent book, *Jihad and Death: The Global Appeal of Islamic State* (2017a), Roy profiles more than 100 jihadis. For many of its followers, Islamic State can "provide a default form of redemption . . . a means of social advancement, or a new identity for Sunnis experiencing a profound crisis. It serves as a foil or useful distraction for its most cynical critics" (Harling, 2014).

At the same time, it responds to the search for strong leadership and clarity of purpose by many who choose to join. They can transform their vulnerability and fear into feeling more masterful and in control of their lives: "once they become jihadists, people fear them . . . once they fear you, they cannot be contemptuous toward you anymore" (Packer, 2015). There also seems to be a personality type among foreign fighters who are more prone to identifying with Islamic State. Many of those who join up are attracted to the brutality of the organisation's message, its strong leadership, and its clarity of purpose. Some of the fighters have the kinds of personalities that need certainty, see the world in black-and-white terms, and cannot tolerate ambiguity or moral complexity. "The Islamic State's ideology exerts powerful sway over a certain subset of the population. Life's hypocrisies and inconsistencies vanish in its face" (Wood, 2015).

Roy claims that the Paris plotters represent most of those who flock to Islamic State: marginal misfits, largely ignorant of religion and geopolitics, and bereft of real historical grievances. "They ride the wave of radical Islam as an outlet for their nihilism because it's the biggest and baddest counter-cultural movement around" (Atran, 2015b). He argues that it is a youth movement that sits outside the influence of parental religion and mainstream culture, but can claim to be rooted in wider youth culture. For him, "this aspect of modern-day jihadism is fundamental – they are in practice more postmodern rather than medieval" (Bellaigue, 2017). "The systematic association with death is one of the keys to understanding today's radicalisation: the nihilist dimension is central. What seduces and fascinates is the idea of pure revolt. Violence is not a means, it is an end in itself" (Roy, 2017b). Freud might well have agreed with some of these ideas.

In the database compiled by Roy on those who have been involved in terrorism in France or who have left France or Belgium to take part in global jihad in the past 20 years, radicals in European countries are

> almost all "born-again" Muslims who, after living a highly secular life – frequenting clubs, drinking alcohol, involvement in petty crime – suddenly renew their religious observance, either individually or in the context of a small group. Most move into action in the months following their religious "reconversion" or "conversion" but have usually already exhibited signs of radicalisation. [Roy, 2017b]

This analysis highlights the difference between the psychological motivation of those fighters who come from Europe as foreign fighters and that of those who joined Islamic State in the Middle East.

The Paris, Brussels, and Manchester attacks

In Britain, part of the horror surrounding the terrorist attacks that took place in France and in Belgium in 2015 and 2016 was the crystallisation of danger at our own back door. Britain was not to remain immune, and in the summer of 2017 it was to be exposed to its own tragic attacks in Manchester and London. Islamist terrorism was no longer a remote threat confined to far-flung and volatile countries in the Middle East and North Africa, but something that could be encountered doing something as simple as sitting in a café or listening to music in the streets of Paris, London, Manchester, or Brussels.

As much as we may wish to search for a clear linear causality, there is no simple interpretation, more like a pot-pourri of complexity. The perpetrators of the attacks did not fit the mould of second-generation immigrant, born to immigrant parents and torn between two identities:

> We're talking about third and fourth-generation [immigrants]; these youngsters are born in Belgium, even their fathers and mothers are born in Belgium, and still they were open for these kinds of messages. . . . A lack of opportunities in Belgium has driven many young men into harm's way because they simply don't feel accepted at home. [Elbagir, Naik, & Laila, 2015]

There were obvious signs of alienation from their societies and a failure to connect with the dominant culture. Presenting as a real problem in France and elsewhere in Europe, many of these people feel disenfranchised both by the country they live in and by their country of origin. Contrast this with the United States, which was built to cope with high levels of immigration:

> In the US, Muslim immigrants attain parity or surpass the average American in wealth and education in the first generation. . . . This is normal in the US, where the second-generation was the President . . . the fourth generation (in Europe) is an IS fighter. . . . In Europe, they are much more likely to be poorer than the average citizen and poorer still after the second generation. [Atran, 2015b]

Barack Obama frequently claimed that

> in no other country is my story even possible. . . . Our Muslim populations, they feel themselves to be Americans. There is, you know, this incredible process of immigration and assimilation that is part of our tradition that is probably our greatest strength. There are parts of Europe in which that's not the case, and that's probably the greatest danger that Europe faces. [Beinart, 2017]

France's defining post-revolutionary philosophy may be incompatible with the modern world.

> In 2004, the French parliament passed a law forbidding religious symbols in public schools. The law emerged in response to Muslim girls coming to class with their hair covered. The legislation affirmed the century-old French concept of *laïcité*, or secularism, prevents religion from intruding into the civic space. . . . French Muslims interpreted the ban as an act of gratuitous hostility. [Packer, 2015]

French culture is monolithic in its presentation: "There can be only one national identity, one national educational system, one version of Frenchness" (Heath, 2015). Yet this would seem to be problematic in a liberal society made up of multiple communities – this imposition of Frenchness can rob the generations of immigrants of a strong clear connection with their culture, which is a significant part of their identity.

In France, 7–8% of the total population is Muslim, the largest percentage of the total population of any state in Europe; at the same time, up to 70% of the prison population is Muslim, which has left an entire underclass of people vulnerable to radicalisation.

> Decayed housing projects, crime, unemployment . . . [the term] *banlieues* has become pejorative, meaning slums dominated by immigrants . . . colossal concrete housing projects built during

the post-war decades, in the Brutalist style of Le Corbusier . . .
became concentrations of poverty and social isolation. . . . The
sense of exclusion in the *banlieues* is an acute problem that the
republic has neglected for decades, but more jobs and better
housing won't put an end to French jihadism. [Packer, 2015]

But the United Kingdom is also having to deal with the challenge of terrorist attacks claimed by Islamic State. In May
2017, a bomb was detonated at a popular music concert by a
British Islamist of Libyan origin, killing 22 people and injur-
ing over a hundred. Many of the casualties were young girls.
Salman Abedi was part of the Libyan community living in
Manchester. His family had spent time in Libya fighting for
an Islamist faction, and young Salman had seen the chaos of
civil war in his home country. He had been exposed to layers
of indoctrination through his father's connections, and in the
mosque he had been absorbing Salafi ideology and theology.

French intelligence suggested he was one of the 3,500
Libyans who later went to fight in Syria. The *Wall Street
Journal* claimed he saw young children dying everywhere;
traumatised by what he saw, he wanted revenge. As an adolescent, he had smoked cannabis, drank, and been involved in
antisocial behaviour. Confused in his identity, he had reacted
violently to Western sexual norms. Rootless and feeling dis-
possessed, caught between the two cultures, he found no sense
of belonging in either country. Through his eyes he saw the
"immorality of the west . . . these seeds became planted and
become extremely toxic" (Stigsgaard Nissen, 2017).

FOUR
The psychology of terrorism

The power of the group

More than 80% of people who join Islamic State do so through personal relationships – mostly through friends, and sometimes through family. Only a minority are recruited by mosques or anonymous strangers (Atran, 2015b). The Paris attackers "lived for a time in the same neighbourhood, some enlisted friends and family members, some moved in the same criminal networks and spent time together in jail" (Atran, 2015b). The group's membership tends to be the same, "brothers, childhood friends, acquaintances from prison, sometimes from a training camp. The number of sets of siblings found is also remarkable" (Roy, 2017b).

Freud outlined his theory of large-group psychology in 1921. He described the "rallying around a leader as one of the crucial elements in the process of synthesising followers into a cohesive group of 'equals' under a leader" (Volkan, 2014, p. 77). Freud's theory of large-group psychology is applicable only to large groups in a regressed state (Waelder, 2007). Here the group takes on a collective large-group identity as if it were a shared skin. At the same time, it weakens the ordinary family bonds (Volkan, 2014, p. 77). A similar pattern of behaviour may be observed with Islamic State, where the power of the groups subsumes all other relationships and weakens the ties of family bonds.

The strength of the group and the intensity of the engagement suggests that the members of the group are prepared to lose their lives for the sake of others. This is the desperate bond between the men who have "chosen to die in battle with their friends rather than to flee on their own and survive" (Junger, 2011, p. 242).

> That bond is the core experience of combat and the only thing you can absolutely count on . . . the shared commitment to safeguard one another's lives is unnegotiable . . . as a soldier, the thing you were most scared of was failing your brothers when they needed you, and compared to that, dying was easy. Dying was over with. Cowardice lingered forever. [Junger, 2011, p. 210]

There is "self-sacrifice in defence of one's community which is virtually universal among humans, extolled in myths and legends all over the world, and undoubtedly ancient" (p. 243). The basic human need is there; combatants, whether fighting for Islamic State or as US soldiers on duty in Afghanistan, are driven by the need "to feel valued and loved by others" (p. 243).

Men form friendships that, while not at all sexual, still contain much of the devotion and intensity of a romance. According to Sebastian Junger (2011, pp. 212–215), in his book *War*, "there was a power and logic to the group that overrode everyone's personal concerns . . . and somewhere in that loss of self could be found relief from the terrible worries about what might befall you". He describes how

> the defence of the tribe is an insanely compelling idea, and
> once you've been exposed to it, there's almost nothing else you'd
> rather do. . . . This commitment to the group is so compelling –
> so addictive, in fact – that eventually it becomes the rationale
> for why the group exists in the first place. [Junger, 2011, p. 214]

One of the factors predicting "willingness to fight is the degree
of fusion with one's comrades" (Webel & Tomass, 2017, p. 221).
"This total fusion leads to a sense of group invincibility and a
willingness of each and every individual in the group to sacri-
fice for each and every other" (Atran, 2015b).

> Not all who fight with the Islamic State are committed zealots
> but when captured Islamic State fighters in Iraq were asked:
> "What is Islam?" they answered: "My life", but they had little
> knowledge of the Quran or hadith, and none of Muslim history.
> Their sense of religion was fused with the vision of a caliphate
> that kills or subjugates any nonbeliever, but their conversion was
> not complete. [Webel & Tomass, 2017, p. 221]

Caught between different identities

The term "identity" is relatively new in psychoanalysis;
Sigmund Freud himself seldom used it. In 1956, the psychoanalyst Erik Erikson described it as "a sustained feeling of
inner sameness within oneself". According to Vamık Volkan
(2014, p. 32), "identity'" refers to a person's subjective experience of him or herself and therefore should be distinguished
from other, related concepts, such as 'character' or 'personality'." This concept of identity is very relevant to the second-
generation European immigrants.

Recent immigration into the United Kingdom has created
a new generation of young people torn in their identity, who
find themselves displaced between the culture of their parents

and that of the country in which they now reside. The countries from which their parents came often have a conservative way of life, particularly around sexual mores, which stand in contrast to the more liberal values in Western countries. There are strict codes of practice, such as not being sexually active until marriage, whereas in the United Kingdom they will have been exposed to a very active sexual youth culture with values that conflict with those of their parents. This will often create a sense of confusion and inner turmoil. Olivier Roy argues that this is a youth movement that sits outside the influence of parental religion and mainstream culture but can claim to be rooted in wider youth culture (Rahim, 2017).

A young mother coming to the United Kingdom from a completely different culture, such as Pakistan, Afghanistan, or Syria, may feel profoundly dislocated and with a deep sense of the loss of support systems that had given security and confidence to her as a parent. The young mother may experience isolation, loneliness, and be unable to speak the language. Her husband may be in the position that, as a recent immigrant, he is not allowed to work, experiencing the humiliation and loss of dignity resulting from this. Such conditions are antithetical to the secure attachment required for healthy parent–child development, and over time the child may feel angry and alienated from his own parents. Some of this behaviour is more likely to be expressed in adolescence, where the attraction of alternative ideas becomes a strong magnet. This offers scope for such extreme ideologies as Islamic State.

According to Vamık Volkan (Volkan & Harris, 1995) many terrorist group members have a history of trauma that can be traced back to early childhood.

Volkan describes how violations of personal boundaries, such as beatings from family members, incest, and other similar events, have contributed to identity problems. They then link their own personal trauma to their perceived persecution by an enemy group.

> Many experience violations of their personal boundaries in the form of beatings by parents, incest, or other such events. Their reactions to these personal traumas later dovetail with their victimisation by an enemy group or their perception of human rights violations inflicted by members of an "occupying" army....
>
> Early or childhood victimisation need not be physical; it can include being abandoned by a mother at an early age, disappointment over being let down by loved ones, a deep sense of personal failure following parental divorce, or rejection by peer groups. [Volkan, 1998, p. 161]

The failure or absence of parenting can be a key factor in creating the conditions for identification with extremism.

> The Kouachi brothers (the Paris bombers) were *fragile* in their makeup – a lack of bearings, a lack of education, a lack of a vision of life, and later that leads to violence – but I don't agree that they were nuts. [Packer, 2015]

> Radicals are in fact often orphans – as the Kouachi brothers were – or come from dysfunctional families. They are not necessarily rebelling against their parents personally, but against what they represent: humiliation, concessions made to society, and what they view as their religious ignorance. [Roy, 2017b]

When the parental figure fails to provide the necessary security for the child, school or peer friendships can act as an alternative family. If these alternatives are not available or fail, this leaves a great sense of confusion, isolation, and profound loneliness. Under these conditions, the young person is at risk of being targeted by Islamic State and "will create a new kind of family hierarchy and morality that interferes with roles within the family (especially women's roles), with normal childhood development, and with the adolescent passage" (Volkan, 2014, p. 61). The identity clash is so taxing and stressful that being presented with a clear political ideology such as Islamic State can be a relief – an easier option – so the individual no longer has to struggle with conflicting ideas and can choose a clear, coherent philosophy.

Social isolation and real or imagined slights collide here: young people who feel they have been wronged or who have suffered in some way develop "flawed personal identities . . . and use their shared ethnic identity as their primary identity" (Volkan, 1998, p. 161). But the danger of this kind of victimhood is that it becomes a trap where it is easier to blame others and deny any responsibility. In this state of denial, "we become done-to, not doers; passive, not active. Blame bars the path to responsibility. The victim, ascribing his condition to others, locates the cause of his situation to outside himself, thus rendering himself incapable of breaking free from his self-created trap" (Sacks, 2015, p. 61). In this state of mind, agency is lost, and the ability to act and take responsibility is diminished. Freud would have argued that turning to a group such as Islamic State can represent the strong father who can rescue the young person from passivity, victimhood, and failure to take control of his own life.

Émile Durkheim may have something of relevance to say here. A French sociologist who wrote in the late nineteenth and early twentieth century, he believed that one of the gravest problems we face in modern times is people's sense of alienation and disconnection from society, which he termed "anomie". Durkheim believed that the strains of modernity and the fast rate of change were creating a crisis over identity. According to Durkheim (1938, pp. 433–440), these phenomena cannot be reduced to biological or psychological grounds, but are due to societal forces and the way society is organised.

Durkheim's central thesis was that the nature of being human leads to an internal struggle between our individual selves and our environment. This creates conflict between our inner selves and the expectations of the group, the latter of which demands commitment and obedience, which can lead to personal conflict (Durkheim, 1893). In consequence, people feel split between the dual existences of society and self. The very nature of the way society is organised stimulates conflict and dissatisfaction. He believed that the roots of these problems lie in an increasing division of labour and rapid social change, which weaken the sense of identification with the wider community. There are immediate links with the current climate of globalisation, which is creating the same kind of splits in society.

> Many of these shocks of modernity were once absorbed by inherited social structures of family and community, and the state's welfare cushions. Today's individuals are directly exposed to them in an age of accelerating competition on uneven playing field. [Mishra, 2017, p. 13]

For many, already vulnerable, this "outsider" identity becomes the chosen identity. Many of these young people will have grown up with the idea that they will never belong. These second-generation immigrants are swimming in a sea of anomie. This internal confusion is then replaced with identification with Islamic State – where moral confusion can be subsumed to clarity of purpose and meaning. But the choice of moral clarity represents the worst and darkest aspects of human behaviour. It is a magnification of the most destructive aspects of human nature. Its aim is to create chaos, stimulate sectarian violence, and draw people into their rigid and savage ideology. They impose a draconian order, enforcing public beheadings, stoning of adulterers, and amputations.

Today, as a result of migration, many people live in cultures that are entirely different from the one their parents had grown up in. Detached from the society in which they live, they are thrown upon their own devices, and they loosen the bonds that had previously tied them to their own culture. People are isolated not only by their heritage, but by living in conditions where deep human connections are being replaced by superficial online communities in which the sense of social disconnect is becoming more entrenched. This disconnect leads to a more solipsistic way of life, at the expense of the community with its common values, morality, beliefs, and normative rules. With the loosening of these common rules, the individual is left adrift, rudderless, in a vacuum. Islamic State has offered some of these young people the clarity of meaning and guidance that is glaringly lacking in twenty-first-century society.

This sense of alienation is then exploited by Islamic State, which, as part of the grooming, will form a strong bond with young Muslims, frequently through the Internet. Islamic State will attempt, when luring young and often vulnerable men and women, to amplify their sense of not belonging and feeling like the outsider. This targeting of the vulnerable in direct online communications works on building the one-on-one personal relationships that many young people feel they are lacking in the real world. This, strengthened by a strong digital message, has allowed Islamic State to become one of the hugely effective online recruiters. Islamic State's recruitment has depended profoundly on their "mastery of modern digital tools, which have transformed the dark arts of making and disseminating propaganda" (Koerner, 2016).

This manipulation by social media creates a narrative of alienation, validating an already negative experience; it can give meaning to the struggle and "*Sturm und Drang*" of adolescence. It is the adolescents' task to seek a sense of identity, a clear route to knowing who they are; this narrative gives clarity. For disenfranchised, more vulnerable young Muslims, this is not about religion, it is about belonging. Within these groups, vulnerable people are not necessarily the most marginalised. They are not necessarily lacking job opportunities.

> The idea that economic deprivation causes young Muslims to become enamoured with terrorist groups was the prevailing theory in the 1980s, but the profiles of recent recruits and some terrorist leaders suggest that thinking has become outdated. Britain has become a breeding ground for extremism as young middle-class Muslims with college degrees and six-figure salaries have flocked to militant groups. [Koplowitz, 2015]

But somewhere within their psychic structure there is a link between exclusion, marginalisation, and humiliation.

Hugo Rifkind wrote about male inferiority and the lure of Islam; he goes as far as to link sexual frustration with violence: "It would be petty to suggest a seething sexual frustration, but come on, we are all thinking it" (2017). Freud would not have been so reticent; he thought that most behaviour was motivated primarily by sexual desire and its frustrations. Rifkind goes on to say, "the marketing pitch of Islamic State itself, is telling Western youth with few prospects that they can be warriors by day and have a harem of slaves by night. Scared of women? Come over here and they can be scared of you." It is a sense of inferiority that may lie at the root of this ugly behaviour, where young men with problems more to do with rootlessness and self-loathing have access to a toxic ideology.

Nearly all recent terrorist activities have been executed by young men who come from Muslim families, thereby conflating Islam with terrorism, but the story is more complex. One of the problems of attempting to apply this broad label of "Islam" is that it cannot possibly describe the behaviour of 1.6 billion people. It is much more nuanced and differentiated, with very different kinds of identity according to the country in which a young person has been brought up: who they are will be shaped by the history of the country, its culture, its economy, and its geography. Islam spans from Indonesia to the Middle East. Very different practices and ways of life are being defined with a broad-brush stroke, which is then magnified by the Western media and its leaders. Such labelling increases the tensions around difference. The experience of young Muslims in the West will be utterly different from, for instance, young Muslims in Bangladesh. Those living in Western countries may feel less confident in their identities, especially if they experience the "War on Terror" and Islamic identity being conflated with terrorism. The general atmosphere and the effects of the terrorist activities of Islamic State and other like-minded groups can create a deepened sense of alienation and reinforce a narrative among the Muslim communities as seeing themselves as outsiders.

Islamic State aims to create tensions and chaos in the West that will seek to destabilise liberal values. Much of their propaganda targets Muslims, telling them that they do not belong and fostering a sense of alienation and disenfranchisement. The conditions are already ripe for this, so the real challenge is how to build and buttress a narrative that is inclusive for Muslims who feel they want to belong. In the United States, strains have been resuscitated "of American political thought – isolationism, xenophobia and even bigotry, particularly against Muslims – that had long been dormant, or at least disreputable, giving national security cover and lifting them from the shadows to the mainstream" (Finer & Mally, 2017). The majority of Americans have now conflated "fundamentalist" as the usual sequel to the word "Muslim" and, in an over-generalised interpretation, have associated both with acts of terrorists. The more accurate picture is, in fact, that fundamentalist groups exist within every faith tradition – including Christianity, Judaism, Islam, Hinduism, Sikhism, Buddhism, and Confucianism.

These extreme right-wing groups have perhaps in many ways objectives similar to such groups as Islamic State, where the essential aim is to challenge the more liberal progressive narrative around coexistence and tolerance for different religions and cultures. A trigger from the environment, such as state-sanctioned animosity, may be the catalyst that propels the traumatised individual towards terrorism. Such conversion comes when a person "believes that passivity will bring further trauma and when he identifies the ethnic garment as his principal tool for dealing with anxiety" (Volkan, 1998, p. 161). In 1990, international relations specialist Katherine Kennedy interviewed 23 state-labelled terrorists or self-proclaimed freedom fighters in Northern Ireland. All of them had experienced trauma in their formative years. One had been beaten by an alcoholic father, another had been sexually molested. "Most had also been humiliated at the hands of their enemies" (Volkan, 1998, p. 161). All of this highlights how the rich brew of alienation among young people who sign up to terrorist groups has been aggravated by a deep sense of disaffection, both in their families and from the state.

The young man, Jamal, was born in London. He was to be one of the early recruits to al Nusra Front, a Salafist jihadist terrorist organisation fighting against Syrian government forces in the Syrian Civil War aiming to establish an Islamic state. He was the youngest child born to a strict, practicing Islamic family and many of his older siblings embraced Islam. Others deviated and expressed themselves through smoking weed, drinking and experimenting with the mores of adolescent western culture. As the youngest child, Jamal was the least engaged with his parents' solid religious belief and Islamic values. He was exposed to the fewest references to the more traditional Islamic cultural values. By the time he was a teenager his siblings had broken the mould of traditional Islamic living, so he grew up in a world with two different sets of values, cultures and practices. By the time he was 18, the crisis of his own identity had become so extreme that when he encountered a group of young men who told him that Muslims were being persecuted and it was his duty to fight for them, he was vulnerable to their influence. There was ultimately such a chasm in terms of his identity between his parents' values and the certainty of the Islamic State ideology, it became the easy way out. He embraced it completely as a way of life as a way of avoiding the pain of being caught between the two conflicting cultures. While it is a normal adolescent milestone to be confused about identity, this takes a more extreme form when there is such as a result of being torn between competing and profoundly different cultures.

What can be done?

One of Freud's seminal messages was that in order to understand the present, we need to understand how the past shaped
the present. His historic contribution was that the earliest
childhood experiences set the foundations for adult behaviour – that early childhood experiences, particularly trauma,
later shape the individual's psychic state. He was interested in
people gaining the insight and self-knowledge to understand
the connection and thereby free themselves of living in the
past; he did not have a great deal to say about the future.

Freud also understood how we might be deceived by
what looked like rational behaviour, as it was often driven by
emotion. He believed that it was essential to get beneath the
defence structures, which, he thought, may take many forms,
such as denial, displacement, distraction, diversion, but, most
of all, not engaging with the serious issue at hand. Freud
recognised that facing the truth meant taking responsibility
for one's own behaviour and action. In war, something similar
happens: it is easier to blame others as being the cause of the
conflict than to look to the part played by one's own side.
Even governments that are not directly involved find it easier
to blame one side without understanding the interactions
between parties involved in the conflict, and how each side
impacts on the other. But what applies to individuals and
families is equally relevant to nations and other groups at
war. History and experience, frustrations, real and imagined
slights, injustices, and outrages influence how nations behave
and react to one another.

For those involved in peace-making, the scars and wounds
of the past will often act as a blockage or an impasse to
imagining a better future. Many of the parties sitting around

a peace table will have been deeply involved in conflict, will have lost members of their families, and may not be in a state of mind to find a compromise. Psychotherapy has much to teach about the creation of safe protected spaces, with the intention of elevating painful emotions to more rational thought. One of the skills psychotherapists have is that they are very carefully trained to listen in a non-judgmental way, enabling the client to express a range of feelings that have previously often felt unacceptable. This equivalent relationship can also be very valuable around the peace table, or on the fringes of it, allowing the building of trust between those who are helping to facilitate the process and their adversaries. It can allow some of the hard questions to be asked and participants to be pushed, which draws on the skills of both psychotherapy and mediation.

Getting into the mindset of the other and what motivates them may be a key component of effectiveness around the peace table. This will require a degree of imagination and empathy – a state of mind often alien to those who have suffered the scars of war. There may, however, be a place for those who are enabling the process to be attuned to the concept of empathy. Empathy is often conflated with sympathy. It is, however, conceptually distinct: while sympathy entails compassion for or affinity with another, empathy does not necessitate either. In conflict resolution, empathy requires understanding the mind of the enemy: the history, trauma, and individual narratives that help to shape their global schema and behaviour. Empathy does not therefore represent agreement or acceptance – rather, a dispassionate consideration of what drives others' behaviour. Despite its roots in psychology, the notion of empathy is politically significant.

Empathy requires understanding the history of Islamic State. How they think and act is likely to be disturbing, as would be their value systems. The challenge is to extend our imagination, not only to those with whom we agree, but even to those who disturb us. Robert Wright argues that "we grant tolerance and understanding to people we see as our friends, and we have a capacity to put ourselves in the shoes of relatives and good friends, and usually lack the ability to put ourselves in the shoes of rivals and enemies" (Wright, 2009, p. 178). We have a tendency to be tolerant of religions, peoples, and cultures with whom we can do business and whose agenda we understand. Conversely, we are often intolerant and belligerent with people whose thinking is opposed to ours. At times, empathy "might be incredibly difficult, witness the extraordinary problems in trying to understand the mindset of the Islamic State. Yet, even that is necessary, for without it there will be little chance of building any peace in Iraq and Syria" (Rogers, 2014).

Psychotherapy, post-Freud, may have much to say here, as he did not have much to say on empathy, and there is a legitimate criticism of his work in that he saw his world through a Western lens. But later theorists understood that one of the core foundation principles is to learn to understand the world through the lens of the person opposite. In the therapist's chair, we spend much time listening, thinking, and imagining what is going on for the person with whom we are working. We are trained to see the world not through our own lens, but through the lens of our clients. Taking this basic idea out of the consulting room and to the peace table becomes an important prerequisite. Of course, this does not need to be done by psychotherapists, but drawing on the training may be relevant here.

Another contribution psychotherapists may have to make is the quality of the relationship and the way it evolves. In the therapy room, the relationship between client and therapist can be a collaborative one, a work in progress. A good therapist will not come in with clever interpretations but will be part of a process, a shared enterprise of learning together. Sometimes they will create new ideas, break old entrenched patterns, and evolve new ways of thinking. This can be equally relevant in issues of war and peace, where new ways of thinking challenge old, tired platitudes and come up with ways of breaking entrenched patterns.

Helping people to change is full of cul-de-sacs, roadblocks, and frustrations. It is a long game; failures and setbacks may be an integral part of the process, not permanent blockages. Often relationships get derailed, off track, hit road blocks – particularly when the client had very deep traumatic experiences and where there is a high level of disturbance. The most important thing in psychotherapy is to stand steady with whoever it is we are working with and assume that it is part of the process. This principle is equally relevant in conflict resolution and preparing people around the peace table, who have experienced the traumas of conflict.

Should we talk to Islamic State?

Freud was a great advocate of dialogue, but he might have differentiated between who you could talk to and who you could not, and between what he may have called psychotic and neurotic mechanisms. Freud originally distinguished between neurosis – the rational part of the mind that suppresses the id, which is the more instinctive part, allowing more rational thought – and psychotic behaviour, which he described as irrational impulses. For him, psychosis was more dominated by the id and was, therefore, more detached from reality.

What Freud believed and had observed from his practice was that those in a neurotic state were more able to create a positive relationship where building trust could be possible. He discouraged psychoanalysts from working with psychosis: he believed that psychotics were more likely to be stuck in a delusional state that was about a false construct and a narrative that bore little familiarity to reality. This distinction could be applied to negotiating with Islamic State, where there will be those who, disturbed by the trauma of war, could be described as being in an equivalent psychotic state. In this hardline and calcified state, there is no room for the compromises of peace-making.

Political leaders are more likely to express abhorrence and threaten declarations of war instead of talking about negotiating with terrorists. Anything less than "war-like rhetoric" looks weak, and seeking to understand appears as an attempt to excuse the behaviour of these groups. So, when political voices suggest that solutions come about through dialogue, the media respond harshly and label such comments as insensitive. It is often out of tune with a public mood hardened by exposure to the brutal methods of Islamic State. For most, negotiation with such a group is unimaginable.

The disturbance and level of suffering created by hardline terrorist groups induces hardline responses by governments, who are more likely to show anger and issue declarations of war than express any desire to understand these groups' motivations. Seeking to understand is seen as an attempt to excuse their behaviour. But there is a pragmatism here, as understanding may lead to better policies that do not feed into the terrorist narrative. Terrorist attacks are terrifying and can never be morally justified. But there might be a place for getting into the mindset of the terrorist, which is not sympathy but may be an essential part of our comprehension.

It can seem grossly insensitive to talk about negotiating with terrorist groups who have actively targeted innocent civilians and used such callous methods. But not to negotiate can cause greater suffering and a greater loss of life. According to Jonathan Powell, who played a pivotal role in the Northern Ireland peace process and now has a specialist role mediating in areas of armed conflict, "we will talk to IS, we always do talk to terrorists, although governments also deny it at the time as they know it is so politically unacceptable" (Powell, 2015).

As a specialist in conflict resolution in the Middle East, I have worked out of the public and media gaze in areas of conflict. This has involved talking to groups that are on the terrorist list, such as Hamas, to better understand their agenda and to explore whether there is scope for a serious dialogue. I am not conflating these groups with Islamic State, whose demands are, on the surface, unpalatable and unacceptable. In broad-brush strokes, Islamic State is a political movement that has world-wide goals, including "the expulsion of non-Muslims from the Arabian Peninsula, the abolishment of the state of Israel, the end of support for dictatorships in Muslim lands" (Wood, 2015). For Western governments these absolutes are non-negotiable, so it would be easy to conclude that there is nothing to speak about. But behind the public rhetoric there may be less hardline agendas, and this needs to be explored.

It is understandable that these groups are seen as pariahs, but my experience is that when you talk to them, you notice the ordinariness of the members; underneath their tough rhetoric it is not a far stretch to imagine that they would want similar things to ourselves: security, taking their children safely to school, visiting their grandmothers. It is difficult to imagine transposing these ideas to Islamic State, whose distasteful methods include beheadings, creating chaos, stimulating sectarian violence, and drawing people into their rigid and savage ideology. Many would consider it both naïve and impossible even to consider negotiating with such groups, giving them an undeserved legitimacy. In July 2016, the Islamic State was unequivocal: "even if you stop bombing us, imprisoning us, torturing us, vilifying us and usurping our lands, we would continue to hate you because the primary reason for hating you will not cease until you embrace Islam." Such statements do not give much hope to negotiators, but there can be a chasm between public rhetoric and private conversations. Hence the importance of quiet contact behind the scenes, to explore whether there is anything to talk about.

It is very difficult to empathise with Islamic State, as their use of violence and nihilistic values has created so much disturbance; yet their behaviour does not come from nowhere: it is the rotten fruit of despair, where people and populations have become deeply disturbed by war. In the horrid and messy complexity of war, ordinary citizens, who are living side-by-side with death, have turned to more extreme jihadi groups for protection.

War is as much about psychological influences as it is about *realpolitik*. As uncomfortable as it may be, it will be necessary to understand the history, the politics, and the religious and cultural meaning of those who have taken on such disturbing identities. It will require looking beyond the political violence and understanding the causes, which may, in some instances, have been marginalisation, de-humanisation, and humiliation. The violence may be seen as a symptom or an autistic communication of some of the very deep grievances in the region.

A deep understanding will be essential, and part of this is to explore and at least consider the possibility of engaging with Islamic State. It will be a tricky and messy process.

Preparations will need to be made quietly behind the scenes. It may involve talking to some of the women's groups, or some of the returnee jihadists, to get a better understanding of the Islamic State's agenda. There will be hardline ideologues in the group, where the chasms are so extreme that negotiations are impossible, but there are always rational actors with whom it is possible to engage.

FIVE
What can we do?

Understanding Islamic State through a political lens is insufficient, and I hope this short but incisive book has managed to identify that understanding human motivation and why people behave in particular ways will make a contribution to the debate. Psychological insight and awareness will be essential. Freud was the founding parent who challenged us to think in this way; but he was concerned with the past and how this affected current human behaviour. He did not see it as within his remit to imagine a better future.

It is, however, within the scope of this book to imagine what could be done. While many of the suggestions are pragmatic, they are primarily influenced by a deep understanding of the human mind and its potential to be both destructive and creative.

1. There is a tendency when terrible things happen to create a culture of fear. It is difficult to have a measured response. It will be important to view the threat of Islamic State in proportion, and governments will need to take responsibility

not to inflame the politics of fear. They do, of course, have responsibilities to protect their citizens, but they can also magnify the threat and create deep polarisation in their societies. The point about proportionality is again reiterated by Oliver Roy when he argues that Islamic State does not mobilise the masses but only draws in those on its fringes:

> there is a temptation to see in Islam a radical ideology that mobilises throngs of people in the Muslim world, just as Nazism was able to mobilise large sections of the German population. But the reality is that IS's pretension to establish a global caliphate is a delusion – that is why it draws in violent youngsters who have delusions of grandeur. [Roy, 2017b]

2. Islamic State has flourished in a culture of 24-hour news. The unadulterated focus on the media and the need to create stories has distorted its impact, has given it more power, and has fed its narrative. The political response needs to be proportionate and seen as one of many responses to some of the threats and challenges in the twenty-first century. Climate change, population growth, water shortage all present much greater challenges, and therefore it is the responsibility of governments to be more measured in their response. Perhaps Margaret Thatcher was right when she deprived the IRA "of the oxygen of publicity on which they depend", invoking "the media to agree among themselves a voluntary code of conduct, a code under which they would not say or show anything which could assist the terrorists' morale or their cause" (Thatcher, 1985).

3. Simultaneously, either the Internet will need to self-regulate, or regulation will become the activity of governments. It has played a key role in creating networks of communities

promoting extremists' behaviour, creating echo chambers of hate speech. Up until now, tech giants such as Facebook and Google have claimed a neutral, moral-free zone. But Facebook's Mark Zuckerberg (2017) has said that it is not enough for social media to be about connection, it now has a moral responsibility to help develop the social infrastructure of communities. In his communication he talked about building supportive and safer communities that were informed, civilly engaged, and inclusive. This technology cannot remain a value-free zone, as consumers are now in this new information ecology. These global companies will need to accept responsibility for the material that is posted on their sites. Without the social media revolution, this global terrorism could not have had the impact it is having. There is now a rich toxic brew of alienated disaffected young people who are vulnerable to being brainwashed and radicalised.

4. The ideological routes of Islam will also need to be revisited – "the root causes of discontent also have to be tackled, especially in the Arab world, and that can only be done by Muslims themselves" (Sawers, 2016). Sharia law will need serious review, as it is part both of the problem and of the solution. Sharia law refers to the body of rules seen to be God's will. At its best, it is about good personal observance, praying five times a day, self-discipline, giving alms to the poor, and long periods of fasting. At its most medieval, Sharia law is brutal and lays out corporal punishments that include chopping off hands, stoning, flogging, and beheading. Islamic scholars recognise the need for revision; they draw a distinction between personal observance and public law and grant greater flexibility over the latter. Reformists recognise the

need to move archaic literalists to a doctrine of inalienable human rights for all the people – a vision desperately lacking in the Middle East.

5. Understanding both the individual and the group motivations of Islamic State and other armed groups will be essential. There are no quick and easy solutions; while military responses may weaken Islamic State in the short term, ultimately ideas cannot be extinguished with bombs. These ideas do not come from nowhere: they emerge out the disturbance of war and the failure to resolve the conflict and to find protection for people. Marginalisation, exclusion, and powerlessness are conditions that motivate some people to look for a hardline ideology that will give clarity of purpose and meaning. A new, comprehensive approach will be required that rethinks the traditional tools of foreign and domestic security and places serious emphasis on a credible and strategic policy of prevention, intervention, and deradicalisation, rather than military intervention.

6. The war against Islamic State has militarily weakened them and deprived them of their so-called state. Time will tell whether it has weakened the idea. Ultimately the root causes that create such movements will need to be addressed; without this, there will only be a sticking plaster on the problem. This will require Western governments to be attuned to where governments and civil society in the Middle East are at, not where we want them to be. As in psychotherapy, we have to bring about change by starting with where people are at, because this is how change happens.

7. The threat of Islamic extremism will remain a generational challenge, and there will be no quick and easy solutions.

Many experts in the field are clear that in terms of domestic policy

> the only real solution is to properly fund interventions at the level of communities, by building robust and trusted partnerships . . . the need for better community policing is perhaps the single intervention most agreed upon by counter-terrorism experts. [Ramsay, 2017]

Here there is need for enormous sensitivity in engaging with local communities and a great deal of listening to how they would tackle their problems. It will have to be a collaborative exercise where new ideas emerge – a shared exercise of learning together. A deeper understanding of how to reduce the sense of anomie and not belonging that these young people caught between these different cultures experience will be essential. Resources are better spent on community integration than on bullets and bombs.

8. It will require a deep consultation process that understands what would help young men and women who are lost in their identities and trapped between different cultures. Careful listening to local communities in order to understand what would help them combat this destructive ideology will be required. Parents, community leaders, and teachers will need to be given the confidence to support each other in challenging young people whom, they fear, they are losing to this poisonous ideology. Current policies, such as the United Kingdom's Prevent Strategy (UK Government, 2011), tend to be more about surveillance than about collaborating with local communities. While the Prevent programme remains controversial, its aim is to tackle the radicalisation that leads to violence. The current programme is criticised for its emphasis on reporting, and

there are allegations of public servants spying on vulnerable young people. Intervention needs to involve community workers, teachers, social workers, and probation officers who "need to start talking on the personal issues that lead individuals to be attracted to violence groups: the power of social networks, the impact of charismatic leaders and young people lacking self esteem and a sense of belonging to the wider society" (Snell, 2017).

9. If contemporary alienation is part of the reason for young men finding themselves drawn to such groups as Islamic State, it will be a real challenge to create a sense of belonging. There will always be angry, alienated young people struggling with their identity – it is part of the adolescent journey to struggle with issues of identity and belonging. But it is worth exploring whether perhaps modern-day jihadism speaks more to post-modern alienation than medieval societies. "Violent extremism represents not the resurgence of traditional cultures, but their collapse, as young people unmoored from millennial traditions flail about in search of a social identity that gives personal significance and glory" (Atran, 2015a).

. . . and, in conclusion

War was central to Freud's thinking, and he recalled "recreating the Napoleonic Wars and lining up his toy soldiers in huge battalions. As an adult, he replaced toy soldiers with his vast collection of 'old and grubby gods'." Many of the figurines in his collection depict the venerated gods and warriors of the ancient world. His favourite among them was Athena, goddess of war, who stood in pride of place at the centre of his desk ("Why War" Exhibition, Freud Museum, 20 Maresfield Gardens, London). But Sigmund Freud and the psychoanalysts he inspired had nothing to say about the predictable future; only the past could be predicted through reconstruction (Philips, 2014b). This is no longer sufficient, and the real challenge is that we depart from the road of mutual self-destruction and use our creativity and imagination to create a safer world.

While Freud had wise thoughts about human nature and its destructive impulses, he did not sufficiently reflect on how to prevent war. He seemed to be prepared to accept the inevitability of the essential destructiveness of human nature. But we cannot resign ourselves to the inevitability of war: we need to do some serious thinking about the emotional, cultural, political, and economic scaffolding that reinforces the infrastructures of conflict. The question to address is: how to militate against creating the conditions for war and to intervene early enough to help mediate tensions and conflict that would benefit not from military responses, but from human ones.

To end with the wise words of Benjamin Ferencz, chief prosecutor at the Nuremberg Trials:

> . . . well, if it's naive to want peace instead of war, let 'em make sure they say I'm naive. Because I want peace instead of war. If they tell me they want war instead of peace, I don't say they're naive, I say they're stupid. Stupid to an incredible degree to send young people out to kill other young people they don't even know, who never did anybody any harm, never harmed them. That is the current system. I am naive? That's insane. [Stahl, 2017]

REFERENCES

Aarts, P., & Roelants, C. (2015). *Saudi Arabia: A Kingdom in Peril*. London: Hurst & Company.

Alderdice, Lord J. (2010a). Off the couch and round the conference table. A. Lemma & M. Patrick (Eds.), *Off the Couch: Contemporary Psychoanalytic Applications*. Oxford: Routledge.

Alderdice, Lord J. (2010b). On the psychology of religious fundamentalism. In: P. J. Verhagen, H. M. van Praag, J. J. Lopez-Ibor Jnr, J. L. Cox, & D. Moussaoui (Eds.), *Religion and Psychiatry: Beyond Boundaries*. Chichester: Wiley Blackwell.

Arendt, H. (1978). *The Life of the Mind*. Boston, MA: Houghton Mifflin Harcourt.

Atran, S. (2015a). Here's what social science says about countering violent extremism. *Huffington Post*, 25 April.

Atran, S. (2015b). ISIS is a revolution. *Aeon*, 15 December.

Atwood, G. E., & Stolorow, R. D. (2014). *Structures of Subjectivity: Explorations in Psychoanalytic Phenomenology and Contextualism*. London: Routledge.

Beinart, P. (2017). Why Trump criticized a London under attack. *The Atlantic*, 4 June.

Bellaigue, C. (2017). Jihad and death by Olivier Roy. Review: The global appeal of Islamic State. *The Guardian*, 21 April.

Breger, L. (2000). *Freud: Darkness in the Midst of Vision*. Oxford: John Wiley & Sons.

Burke, J. (2017). After Islamic State – Collapse may come swiftly but will it leave the world any safer? *Prospect Magazine*, May.

Dostoyevsky, F. (1880). *Brothers Karamazov*. New York: Simon and Schuster.

Durkheim, É. (1893). *The Division of Labor in Society*, trans. W. Hall. New York: Free Press.

Durkheim, É. (1938). Social facts. In: M. Martin & L. C. McIntyre (Eds.), *Readings in the Philosophy of Social Science*. Boston, MA: MIT Press, 1994.

Einstein, A., & Freud, S. (1933). *Why War?* International Institute of Intellectual Co-Operation, League of Nations. Available at: http://thecastsite.com/grandma/MOVE/Backups/philosophy.thecastsite.com/readings/einstein1.pdf

Elbagir, N., Naik, B., & Laila, B. A. (2015). Why Belgium is Europe's front line in the war on terror. *CNN*, 24 March.

Erikson, E. (1956). The problem of ego identification. *Jourtnal of the American Psychoanalytic Asociation, 4*: 56–121.

Fakhry Davids, M. (2011). *Internal Racism: A Psychoanalytic Approach to Race and Difference*. Basingstoke: Palgrave Macmillan.

Fiebig-von Has, R., & Lehmkuhl, U. (1997). *Enemy Images in American History*. Oxford: Berghahn Books.

Finer, J., & Malley, R. (2017). How our strategy against terrorism gave us Trump. *New York Times*, 4 March.

Freud, S. (1900a). *The Interpretation of Dreams. S.E., 4 & 5*.

Freud, S. (1901b). *The Psychopathology of Everyday Life. S.E., 6*.

Freud, S. (1915b). Thoughts for the times on war and death. *Collected Papers*. London: Hogarth Press, 1953.

Freud, S. (1921). *Group Psychology and the Analysis of the Ego. S.E., 18*.

Freud, S. (1927c). *The Future of an Illusion. S.E., 14*: 3.

Freud, S. (1930a): *Civilization and Its Discontents. S.E., 21*: 59.

Freud, S. (1947). *On War, Sex and Neurosis*. New York: Arts & Science Press.

Freud, S. (1954). *The Origins of Psycho-Analysis: Letters to Wilhelm Fliess, Drafts and Notes: 1887–1902*, ed. M. Bonaparte, A. Freud, & K. Ernst; trans E. Mosbacher, & J. Strachey. New York: Basic Books, 1954.

Freud, S., & Freud, A. (2001). *Complete Psychological Works of Sigmund Freud. Vol. 1*. London: Random House.

Fritz, C. E. (1961). Disaster. In: R. K. Merton & R. A. Nisbet (Eds.), *Contemporary Social Problems*. New York: Harcourt, 1976.

Goldin, I., & Kutarna, C. (2016). In an age of discovery, it takes real guts to be optimistic. *Huffington Post*, May.

Grayling, A. C. (2017). *War: An Enquiry*. New Haven, CT: Yale University Press.

Grossman, D. (1996). *On Killing: The Psychological Cost of Learning to Kill in War and Society*. New York: Back Bay Books.

Haney, C., Banks, C., & Zimbardo, P. (1973). A study of prisoners and guards in a simulated prison. *Naval Research Reviews, 26* (9): 1–17.

Harling, P. (2014). IS back in business. *Le Monde Diplomatique*, September.

Heath, A. (2015). France's grim estates are the perfect breeding grounds for terrorism. *The Telegraph*, 18 November.

Hidayatullah, A. (2003). Islamic conceptions of sexuality. In D. W. Machacek & M. M. Wilcox, *Sexuality and the World's Religions* (pp. 255–292). Santa Barbara, CA: ABC-CLIO.

Hobbes, T. (1651). *Leviathan*. Oxford: Clarendon Press, 1984.

Hollis, R. (2015). After the UN Security Council vote, the West must heed the lessons of Iraq. *The Guardian*, 22 November.

Junger, S. (2011). *War*. London: Fourth Estate.

Junger, S. (2016). *Tribe: On Homecoming and Belonging*. London: Fourth Estate.

Kahr, B. (2017). *Psychotherapy Is Not a Spectator Sport: The Dissemination of Psychoanalysis from Freud to Orbach.* Paper presented at Psychotherapy Is a Cultural Issue: The Influence of Susie Orbach's Work on Theory, Practice and Values conference, 22 April.

Kaldor, M., & Turkmani, R. (2015). Why we should oppose British air strikes against ISIL in Syria. *Open Democracy,* 27 November.

Koerner, B. (2016). Why ISIS is winning the social media war. *WIRED,* April.

Kogan, I. (2007). *The Struggle against Mourning.* New York: Jason Aronson.

Koplowitz, H. (2015). Islamic extremism in Europe: Is high youth unemployment to blame? *IB Times,* 14 January.

Levy, B. (2008). *Left in Dark Times: A Stand against the New Barbarism.* New York: Random House.

Livesey, T. (2015). *The Islamic State: Who Are They and What Do They Want?* Oxford Research Group. Unpublished paper, November.

Lomas, D. (2000). *The Haunted Self: Surrealism, Psychoanalysis, Subjectivity.* New Haven, CT: Yale University Press.

Marr, A. (2009). *The Making of Modern Britain.* London: Macmillan.

Martinez, R. (2016). *Creating Freedom: Power, Control and the Fight for Our Future.* Edinburgh: Canongate Books.

Milgram, S. (1963). Behavioral study of obedience. *Journal of Abnormal and Social Psychology, 67* (4).

Mishra, P. (2015). How to think about Islamic State. *The Guardian,* 24 July.

Mishra, P. (2017). *Age of Anger: A History of the Present.* London: Allen Lane.

Monbiot, G. (2015). *Surgical Strike.* www.monbiot.com/2015/10/09/surgical-strike

Moubayed, S. (2015). *Under the Black Flag: At the Frontier of the New Jihad.* London: IB Tauris.

Opotow, S. (1990). Moral exclusion and injustice: An introduction. *Journal of Social Issues, 46* (No. 1, Spring), 1–20.

Packer, G. (2015). The other France: Are the suburbs of Paris incubators of terrorism? *The New Yorker*, 31 August.

Peeble, G. (2017). The rise of anxiety in the age of inequality. *OpenDemocracy*, 20 May.

Philips, A. (2014a). *Becoming Freud: The Making of a Psychoanalyst.* New Haven, CT: Yale University Press.

Philips, A. (2014b). Rethinking Freud. *Life, Art and Therapy* [Podcast], July.

Pick, D. (2012). *The Pursuit of the Nazi Mind: Hitler, Hess, and the Analysts.* Oxford: Oxford University Press.

Pinker, S. (2011). *The Better Angels of Our Nature: The Decline of Violence in History and Its Causes.* London: Allen Lane.

Powell, J. (2015). Bombing Isis is not enough: We'll need to talk to them too. *The Guardian*, 1 December.

Rahim, S. (2017). Books in brief: *Jihad and Death*, by Oliver Roy. *Prospect Magazine,* May.

Ralston, S. (1992). *Voltaire's Bastards: The Dictatorship of Reason in the West.* New York: First Vintage Books.

Ramsay, G. (2017). No, the link between terrorism and our foreign policy isn't simple. *OpenDemocracy*, May.

Rifkind, G., & Picco, G. (2014). *Fog of Peace: The Human Face of Conflict Resolution.* London: I.B. Tauris.

Rifkind, G., Picco, G., & Wilson, P. (2014). *Conflict Prevention & Early Intervention: A Credible Team of Mediators.* Oxford Research Group, May.

Rifkind, H. (2017). Male inferiority and the lure of Jihadism. *The Times*, 6 June.

Rogers, P. (2014). Through the fog of peace. *OpenDemocracy*, 8 September.

Roy, O. (2017a). *Jihad and Death: The Global Appeal of Islamic State.* London: Hurst.

Roy, O. (2017b). Who are the new Jihadis? *The Guardian*, 13 April.

Sacks, J. (2015). *Not in God's Name: Confronting Religious Violence.* London: Hodder & Stoughton.

Sawers, J. (2016). ISIS is down but not yet out. *Financial Times*, 2 September.

Singer, P. (1981). *The Expanding Circle*. Oxford: Clarendon Press.

Snell, A. (2017). Prevent should stop fixating on Islam. *Prospect*, July.

Stahl, L. (2017). What the last Nuremberg prosecutor alive wants the world to know. *CBS News*, 7 May.

Stigsgaard Nissen, L. (2017). Inside ISIS: The making of a radical. *The Guardian*, 28 May.

Thatcher, M. (1985). "We must try to find ways to starve the terrorist and the hijacker of the oxygen of publicity on which they depend." Speech to American Bar Association, South Kensington, Central London, 15 July.

UK Government (2011). *Prevent Strategy*. Available at www.gov.uk/government/publications/prevent-strategy-2011

Volkan, V. (1998). *Blood Lines: From Ethnic Pride to Ethnic Terrorism*. Boulder, CO: Basic Books.

Volkan, V. (2014). *Blind Trust: Large Groups and Their Leaders in Times of Crisis and Terror*. Charlottesville, VA: Pitchstone.

Volkan, V., & Harris, M. (1995). The psychodynamics of ethnic terrorism. *International Journal of Minority and Group Rights*, *3* (2).

Waelder, R. (2007). The principle of multiple function: Observation on over-determination. *Psychoanalytic Quarterly*, *76* (1).

Ward, C. (2017). Syria and the Western Jihadi: Tales from the Front. The Walter S. Gubelmann Memorial Lecture. *Four Arts*, 28 March.

Webel, R., & Tomass, M. (Eds.). (2017). *Assessing the War on Terror: Western and Middle Eastern Perspectives*. London: Routledge.

Weiss, M., & Hassan, H. (2015). *ISIS: Inside the Army of Terror*. New York: Regan Arts.

Weizman, E. (2011). *The Least of All Possible Evils: Humanitarian Violence from Arendt to Gaza*. London: Verso.

Whitebook, J. (2017). *Freud: An Intellectual Biography*. Cambridge: Cambridge University Press.

Wilkinson, R. G. (2006). The impact of inequality. *Social Research, 73* (2): 711–732.

Wood, G. (2015). What ISIS really wants. *The Atlantic,* March.

Wright, R. (2009). *The Evolution of God: The Origins of Our Beliefs.* London: Little Brown.

Yazbek, S., Gowanlock, N., & Ahmedzai Kemp, R. (2016). *The Crossing: My Journey to the Shattered Heart of Syria.* London: Random House.

Yovel, Y. (1992). *Spinoza and Other Heretics, Vol. II: Adventures in Immanence.* Princeton, NJ: Princeton University Press.

Zuckerberg, M. (2017). Building global community [Facebook post, 16 February]. Retrieved from https://www.facebook.com/notes/mark-zuckerberg/building-global-community/10154544292806634/